Michael

BAROQUE
IN ITALY

1   *The Superga, Turin (1718–31)*
Filippo Juvara, architect

BAROQUE
IN ITALY

James Lees-Milne

B. T. BATSFORD LTD LONDON

First Published 1959

MADE AND PRINTED IN ENGLAND BY
WILLIAM CLOWES AND SONS LTD, LONDON AND BECCLES
FOR THE PUBLISHERS

B. T. BATSFORD LTD

4 FITZHARDINGE STREET, PORTMAN SQUARE, LONDON W1

PREFACE

It hardly seems necessary to point out that a mere two hundred pages can only skim the surface of the complicated Italian Baroque. They cannot go deep or far. This volume must be regarded then as a rather cursory and partial introduction to the subject. In writing it I have endeavoured to investigate the origin and meaning of a great phase of classical art, which initiated in Rome, spread in the course of a century and a half across Europe and Latin America. A second volume, *Baroque in Spain and Portugal* will, I hope, continue the story in the same general terms a stage further.

Future students of the Italian Baroque, in all its manifestations, will have an advantage over me. They will be able to refer to a book that has only recently been published. This is Rudolph Wittkower's *Art and Architecture in Italy, 1600–1750*, a comprehensive work of immense erudition and, in so far as such a thing is possible, of finality upon the subject.

I am much indebted to two friends. Miss Dorothy Margaret Stuart read through my typescript. Father Illtud Evans, O.P. read through the proofs. Both have given me invaluable help.

J. L.-M.

*"We cannot understand an age
till by the comparison of one art with another
we find its spirit."*

Anon. TIMES LITERARY SUPPLEMENT, 1927

CONTENTS

ACKNOWLEDGMENT

THE Author and Publishers wish to thank the following for permission to include the illustrations appearing in this book:

Accademia, Florence, for fig. 3

Alinari, Rome, for figs. 4, 6, 7, 10–12, 17, 30, 34, 43, 45, 62, 63, 66, 71, 73, 77, 78 and 80

American School of Classical Studies at Athens, for fig. 20

Anderson, Rome, for figs. 1, 2, 8, 9, 16, 18, 19, 21, 26, 27, 29, 31–3, 35–8, 40, 42, 44, 47, 48, 51–6, 61, 64, 65, 67, 72, 75 and 79

Burlington Magazine, for fig. 39

Editions S.L., Lyon, for fig. 41

Ian Graham, for fig. 60

A. F. Kersting, F.R.P.S., for figs. 23, 46, 59, 69 and 74

The Mansell Collection, for figs. 1, 2, 4, 8–12, 16, 18, 19, 21, 26, 27, 29–38, 40, 42–5, 47, 48, 51–6, 61–7, 71–3, 75 and 77–80

Naya, Venice, for fig 5.

LIST OF ILLUSTRATIONS

The numerals in parentheses in the text refer to the *figure numbers* of the illustrations

11

1. Mannerism

THE golden age of Rome's High Renaissance was virtually doomed on the feast of All Saints, 1517. On that inauspicious day Martin Luther appended his ninety-five theses to a church door in Wittenberg. Thus the first nails were hammered into the coffin of that once-smiling humanism which for two centuries had irradiated the Christian Church. Exactly ten years later the sack of Rome by the Imperial troops of Charles V came as a second blow of illimitable consequence to European culture. Thereafter for seven or eight years complete dislocation of all intellectual activity ensued in the very heart of western civilization. During the turmoil Germany, half Switzerland, all Scandinavia and then England, were lost to Catholicism. In the eyes of the apostates freedom of the individual was now to be identified with the Reformation; but in fact the split in Christendom soon led to a belief in a restricting nationalism which has persisted ever since. The immediate period of conflict was of course temporary. It was a tragic period, one of frustration and despair. It had an inevitable effect upon the arts. It threw them into one of those recurrent melting pots of history. The group of Bramante's and Raphael's followers in Rome was scattered.[1] Sanmicheli fled to Verona, Sansovino to Venice, Pierino del Vaga to Genoa and Parmigianino to Bologna. Michelangelo, who was at this time in Florence, abandoned art for politics and the urgent military defence of his native city. The havoc wrought by the sack of Rome took at least three-quarters of a century to obliterate, and the ultimate settlement saw the vision of artists completely changed from that of the long and comparatively quiescent days before 1527.

[1] N. Pevsner, "The Architecture of Mannerism", *The Mint*, 1946.

Throughout the remainder of the sixteenth century the Catholic Church was slowly reassembling its spent forces. In Rome after the sack a process of clearing up and restoration was at once begun. Churches were rebuilt as much for economic reasons and to restore confidence as for spiritual motives. The faithful could be relied upon to contribute generously. By this artificial means employment was provided and the trades were restarted. But politically and economically Rome was for a time obliged to rely for its physical survival upon victorious Spain. This bondage had a deleterious influence upon thought and art. Some of the most unlikeable and none of the most agreeable Spanish characteristics imposed themselves upon the Italian way of life. The ecclesiastical authoritarianism of the Middle Ages returned, strengthened by the borrowed methods of the Spanish Inquisition and by the emphasis of Jesuit theology. Life in the peninsula became grim indeed.

The worldly joys of the Renaissance were temporarily laid aside. Outward display was abandoned. The Counter-reformation was a time of extreme sadness and gravity of manners, accompanied by exterior signs of piety, and a parade of contrition and frequent confession, as though thereby to combat the menace of Protestantism. Ornament and colour so dear to the Italians were now regarded as demoralizing. Because in Bologna the mournful Charles V was invariably dressed in black velvet, with black silk stockings, black shoes, a black cap and black feathers, and only the sparsest relief of jewellery upon his person, the impressionable Italian upper classes followed this fashion. In architecture too the lugubrious trend was reflected in a paucity of ornament. Another distressing habit adopted by Italian aristocrats from the Spaniards was *hidalgoism*. Hitherto their great strength had been that they were never idle. Throughout the peninsula, and particularly in Venice, Pisa and Genoa, it was not considered derogatory for gentlemen to take to commerce. On the contrary work was deemed to enhance the honour of an ancient lineage. Thus during the Renaissance closer relations had existed between the classes in Italy than at any period and in any country before the twentieth century. We have an example of the new *hidalgoism* and the wretchedness it brought about in the absurd situation of Michelangelo's father. He was so poor a gentleman that he could barely live on the income from his meagre estates. Yet he actually boasted that he never stooped to augment it by looking for employment. His son who was eventually obliged to support his father—and his brothers—had the greatest difficulty in winning parental consent to his becoming an artist.

The course of the Counter-reformation was to a large extent determined by the decrees of the Council of Trent. That these decrees had not flowed in a spontaneous stream from the Vatican but were wrung from it drop by drop is indicated by the fact that the very mention of the Council was always an abomination to successive pontiffs. The Emperor Charles V, half Spanish in blood, was its instigator in the face of opposition from Paul III, who had wanted to put condemnation of Protestantism before the reform of abuses. Although the Council was officially opened in 1542, a calculated procrastination prevented it from achieving anything for the first twenty years of its being. It was then reopened by Pius IV, Gian Angelo Medici, a benevolent, pleasure-loving but diplomatic Pope, who because of these very qualities achieved in a short time what a more determined and ruthless man might have failed to do.

It is a mistake to attribute to the Council too much adverse influence upon the arts. It is undeniable that a few Tridentine[1] decrees affected them indirectly and not too happily. There was that famous decree of 1563 proscribing all images which might inspire erroneous doctrines and suggest impurity and indeed anything uncustomary. Furthermore the nude was to be totally forbidden in the representation of any religious subject. This particular injunction was from time to time remembered by scrupulous individuals like Clement VIII, who all but effaced the Last Judgement, and Clement IX, who provided a metal tunic for the naked figure of Truth on his predecessor's monument in St. Peter's. "Whereas Truth usually pleases too little", observed an irreverent contemporary, "here she

[1] Pertaining to the Council of Trent.

has pleased too much." On the other hand the representation of mythological subjects was tolerated by tacit understanding, provided it was kept outside sacred premises. Even Cardinal (later Saint) Charles Borromeo caused to be erected in Bologna a colossal and nude image of Neptune as a fountain, and Cardinal Odoardo Farnese chose for the painted ceilings of his palace in Rome subjects of undisguisedly profane character.

Certainly the Church did not become a tyrannical dictator of artists after the Council of Trent[1]. It was never even as severe with them as it set out to be. It did not condemn Renaissance Humanism; it merely sought to put back decency into religious art. Naturally it directed artists into the way it wished its commissions to be carried out, just as today a commercial firm will outline the subject and even the design of a mural composition required for a board-room. And, after all, religion remained the common inspiration of most artists until well within the eighteenth century. The story of the Inquisition summoning Veronese in 1573 to defend a painting and obliging him to alter it is often quoted because it was an isolated instance. It is not a creditable story, but at least the distinguished painter was released after his apology for having introduced such profane subjects as dwarfs, buffoons, dogs and courtesans. St. Charles Borromeo likewise made an abortive attempt to regularize the planning of churches. The circle and the Greek cross were to be discarded; only the Latin cross was to be retained because it was truly emblematic of our Lord's Passion; doorways were no longer to be round-headed, which was pagan, but square, which for some recondite reason was considered unexceptionable for a Christian edifice. But these decrees had no effect whatsoever. Such reactionary

[1] Counter-reformation obscurantism had a far more disastrous effect upon learning. The Index prevented Universities taking up new philosophies and sciences for fear of heresy. A student of Rome University complained to his parents that hardly any subjects were taught at all and that to pass away the time the professors would open discussions on the merits of unnatural vice. Clement VIII issued a bull in 1595 forbidding Italians to travel abroad except under the most stringent conditions. Queen Elizabeth of course put a similar prohibition upon her subjects for fear of their conversion to Papacy.

endeavours could not last for long. Besides, as a consequence of the
victory of Lepanto over the infidel Turk a new self-confidence was
established in the Vatican. Gradually the Church could afford to
modify its uncompromising code. It adopted new tactics. Borromeo,
whose zealous faith at least did not take a puritanical form,
advocated sumptuous ceremonial, of which the Jesuits of the succeeding century were past masters, believing that the quickest way to
salvation was through visual pleasures.

The Counter-reformation meant to preserve the *status quo*. In this
respect it was unlike the Renaissance and Reformation with their
opposing yet positive ideals. It was no more than a bulwark to defend the Catholic Faith, as the very name given it by posterity
implies. It was a great movement but did not provide a positive
formula to inspire hopes of a newer and better world. The Counter-
reformation reaffirmed practical, intellectual and ethical values. Perhaps it was unromantic, but it was necessary and on the whole
beneficial.

The Reformation on the other hand, unlike the old Renaissance
Humanism which had been an aristocratic rather than a democratic
symptom, was ostensibly in the interests of the people. Inevitably,
however, it retarded their development. It did not bring a much-
vaunted liberty and tolerance either in a spiritual or a political
sense but set up other tyrants worse than Popes and Kings. In lands
where the Reformation prevailed the old rulers were eclipsed by
state-controlled churches; and despotic government by a new
plutocracy was introduced. Far from bringing peace the Reformation
caused prolonged religious warfare and political disunion which only
the Spanish peninsula was spared. The Counter-reformation policy
proved in the long run wiser and sounder, for its diplomacy was more
adroit. It may not have encouraged new sciences nor even have
evolved a new Humanism; but it did not jettison the Renaissance
culture. On the contrary it fostered it and what it termed "the
correct style" to which the Reformation had been bitterly and
irrationally opposed. For in defying the Renaissance standards of
classical beauty the Reformation had sought to detract from them

by mockery. Thus in painting we have Rembrandt's deliberate uglification of the female nude as a show of protest. The new Protestantism was joyless and harsh. In the northern countries it was responsible for that formless and uncomfortable style of architecture notorious in Flanders and Northern Germany.

The very nature of the Counter-reformation—intrinsically political, and conservative as it was—accounts for its small intellectual and artistic harvest. No great work of prose was the outcome of its policy: no great poetry but Tasso's, and he was not a poet of passion, humour, nobility of action or even of particular piety, but of a new and hitherto undefined emotion called sentiment. The sensuous melancholy of his *Aminta* was not such as to commend it to the Church. His *Gerusalemme Liberata,* because it celebrated the triumph of the Church over paganism, was accepted purely for its propaganda value. The Counter-reformation produced no great liturgical music. This particular art remained at a very low ebb. Current Masses still bore titles adopted from popular Flemish melodies, such as *Adieu mes Amours, Baisse-moi* and *Le Vilain Jaloux* of which the words were often frankly obscene. Their performance in St. Peter's was usually pitiable. The choir rivalled the orchestra, the tenor the bass, the organ the viol, so that the accumulated din was compared by one contemporary to that of "a stye of grunting pigs" or "the squalling of cats in January". True, the Council of Trent investigated the scandal and ordained that what it termed impure or lascivious music in the house of God be forbidden. This decree was unexceptionable. But it was touch and go whether polyphonic music in churches should be prohibited altogether. Palestrina (1525–94), the greatest composer of the age, fortunately averted the threat by submitting to St. Charles Borromeo three Masses which won the approval of the Church Commissioners. Although patronized and employed by the Papacy, Palestrina was great not because but in spite of the Counter-reformation. Nevertheless, such was the force of the ensuing Baroque movement that within a quarter of a century after his death his beautiful Masses written for unaccompanied voices were relegated to the archives.

As for painting, sculpture and architecture they certainly did not flourish in Rome because of the Counter-reformation, and, as we are about to see, those artists who achieved renown were chiefly impelled by a mood of protest. The outcome of the Council of Trent was not then a burst of artistic inspiration any more than it was an asphyxiation of genius. But it did mean the re-emergence of the Papacy as a secular and spiritual power more formidable than ever before in its history. Because of the Council papal prestige was immensely enhanced.

THE MEANING OF THE TERM—MANNERISM: FIRST APPLIED TO PAINTING

The new expression of art in this difficult era of revolt is now called Mannerism. It marks the end of Renaissance serenity. Until the beginning of the twentieth century the movement succeeding the Renaissance was loosely termed "Baroque". Any sixteenth-century work of art that was irregular, tortured or bizarre was so denominated. Heinrich Wölfflin[1] as long ago as 1888 was the first historian to recognize that after 1520 no work of art was purely Renaissance, and he postulated that by about 1580 the Baroque style was clearly indicated. By the 1920s German scholars perceived that within the period adumbrated by Wölfflin and even beyond it (that is to say until at least the end of the sixteenth century), Italian art lacked one trait common to art before 1520 and after 1600, namely a confidence and robustness coincidental with normal acceptance of the Church's teaching. Max Dvorak[2] was the first to define the whole of this interim period as "Mannerist". Perhaps the most comprehensive explanation of Mannerism to be given in English is Nikolaus Pevsner's essay published in 1946.[3] Even so there are grounds for disagreeing with Dr. Pevsner's thesis that the Reformation was the sole impetus behind Mannerism and that the Counter-reformation was a revulsion from Renaissance paganism. On the contrary

[1] H. Wölfflin, *Renaissance und Barock*, 1888.
[2] M. Dvorak, "Greco und der Manierismus," *Kunstgeschichte als Geistesgeschichte*, 1924.
[3] N. Pevsner, "The Architecture of Mannerism", *The Mint*, 1946.

Mannerism was engendered before the Reformation was regarded by the Church as a serious menace; and the Counter-reformation, although, as its name implies, the practical and intellectual opponent of the Reformation, was not hostile to Renaissance paganism with which in a sense it actually allied itself.

Today the word Mannerism implies more than a studied affectation. Mannerist art, says Pevsner, is indeed self-conscious and stiff. Centuries earlier, Vasari, a contemporary of the movement under discussion, criticized the prevalent style of Florentine painting for being *di maniera* and not *di natura*. He doubtless had in mind artists like Pontormo and Pontormo's follower, Bronzino, whose secular paintings were characterized by lack of naturalism and built up by a series of formal groupings of which the subjects were usually allegorical. A more flagrant illustration of the anti-naturalism which Vasari might have inveighed against, had he known it, is found in the school of painting at Fontainebleau, which became the centre of a transalpine Mannerism. Here under the patronage of the Valois Kings the style flourished in its most extravagant form. Its protagonists were Rosso and Primaticcio, Italians who had left their native regions on account of the disturbed conditions. Although usually so lavish in praise of his contemporaries, Vasari yet hinted that in his lifetime art was beginning to decline. This was during the late 1560s after the death of Michelangelo, whom he accounted the greatest artist of modern times; and so his views, however just, are understandably pessimistic. Giuliano Briganti[1] points out that Vasari constantly used the expression *lo sforzato*—the strained effect—which he observed to be creeping into his contemporaries' style of painting, and that by this expression he was obliquely but unconsciously indicating Mannerism.

Briganti traces the first signs of Mannerism back to the second decade of the sixteenth century. He categorically associates it with a group of young Tuscan painters, Beccafumi, Pontormo and Rosso, who had revolted against the strict classicism of Raphael and his disciples engaged between the years 1509 and 1513 upon the decoration of the Stanze at the Vatican. Beccafumi was already painting

---

[1] Giuliano Briganti, *Il Manierismo*, 1945.

in 1512 in an entirely novel manner which was both tormented and dramatic. That very year witnessed the completion of Michelangelo's Sistine Chapel ceiling, which Beccafumi must have seen in progress while on a visit to Rome. In the Academy at Siena are cartoons by Beccafumi for the Cathedral pavement (2). These Old Testament scenes are distraught and violent and composed of a practically unco-ordinated series of detail. The influence of Michelangelo is distinctly apparent in them.

Now Vasari noted how Pontormo working in Florence about this time was deliberately imitating the engravings and intaglios of Dürer. In other words during a period of dominant classicism in Italy the Nordic spirit from Germany was exercising more than a casual influence upon Tuscan painting. Here is another aetiological factor in the history of Mannerism to be taken into consideration, well before disaster was to break loose upon Christendom. Briganti, however, advances no other explanation of the volte-face from classicism than *il vagare di un sentimento irrequieto, solitario, inappagato*. But sentiments of restlessness and dissatisfaction afflict every healthy generation of young men and are not peculiar to the first generation of Mannerists. We must look for the explanation in a combination of circumstances. To a fervent belief that the idyllic serenity of Raphael's art as expressed in the Stanze was by now quite outworn and outmoded were later added the profound political and religious disturbances beginning to rock Italy. It is surely not surprising that a new generation of artists was highly sensitive to such changes. In times of chaos artists stress supernatural rather than human elements: for inspiration and theme they plumb not the senses but the intellect and the soul. Hence the clarity of Renaissance form and composition now counted for nothing. Liberties were taken with the human shape. Michelangelo broadened it so as to emphasize man's physical tragedy: El Greco elongated it in order to express spiritual fervour. A contradiction of the usual physical functions resulted. Not only were the proportions of the body disregarded but those of buildings likewise. Weight was not apparently sustained where support was to be expected. Dramatic motifs proliferated throughout composition. A seeming delight was evident in discordant patterns.

By the end of the sixteenth century Roman painters no longer belonged to a school. Individuals were working indiscriminately along feeble Michelangelesque lines and, simultaneously, along Raphaelesque lines, so contradictory had their work become. The influence of the Vatican Loggie grotesques had, in Briganti's words, by now become "part of the cultural luggage of Mannerism". Men like Taddeo Zucchero and, better known still, Giuseppe Cesari (d'Arpino), with his slick, mechanical talent, were the leading exponents of the *stile Manieroso*.[1] Mannerist painting had become the universal language whose form was stilted and conventional. In Rome it had assumed an essentially decorative quality at the service of architecture. It was characterized by little scenes of landscape or mythology practically suffocated and unobserved within a welter of geometrical stucco compartments on frieze and ceiling. Indeed the Mannerist epoch saw a notable advance in decoration. The importance to society of the decorative artist was acknowledged by the foundation in 1577 of the Academy of St. Luke.

ARCHITECTURE AND MICHELANGELO (1474–1563)

"The High Renaissance worked within such narrow limits that there was an ever-present danger of self-exhaustion."[2] This threat must assail any movement which has ultimately expressed all the moods within its repertory of thought and sentiment. The logical precision of Bramante's architecture, such as his Tempietto at S. Pietro in Montorio (which one hundred years earlier Brunelleschi had predicted in the Pazzi Chapel), was by the very nature of time and man's unquenchable thirst for fresh sources of inspiration now considered dull and unsatisfactory. To determine whether the resulting change of style was for better or worse is purely academic and a matter of taste. It is incontrovertible that Mannerist architecture in, let us say,

---

[1] Pietro da Cortona used these words of Cesari's painting.
[2] H. Wölfflin, *Renaissance und Barock*, 1888.

3 *One of Michelangelo's Captives, intended for the tomb of Pope Julius II (Accademia, Florence)*

4 *Villa Pia, Vatican Gardens (1561)*
Pirro Ligorio, architect

5 *The Zecca, Venice (1536)*
J. Sansovino, architect

the Biblioteca Laurenziana, Florence (7), or the Villa Pia in the Vatican gardens (4), is a direct contradiction of the style that went before. The spirit of these buildings conveys to us doubt, conflict and a desire to flaunt. Unquestionably where Bramante resolved physical obstacles with a mathematical simplicity Michelangelo and Pirro Ligorio deliberately exploit broken surfaces and so shock by intentional malformations. We have to wait for the Baroque to reunite surfaces in rhythmical, unbroken sweeps so as to provide continuous changes of aspect with every change of viewpoint—one of the distinguishing contributions of the seventeenth century to the science of architectural siting.

What then are the chief physical characteristics of Mannerist architecture? A Mannerist façade is composed of separate, often disparate units, each a complete end in itself. A façade does not set out to be a unified whole. A second characteristic is observable in the Mannerist interior. Whereas decoration of the High Renaissance, and for that matter of the Baroque, never intrudes upon the architecture but remains subordinate to it, Mannerist decoration intrudes all the time without, however, assuming a very successful rôle in its own right. At the same time the old fifteenth-century love of colour— to be revived in the seventeenth—was subdued in favour of a generally monochrome treatment deemed suitable to the gravity of the architecture it was meant to enhance. The minor art of decoration was not again to be so dominant until the reign of the Rococo in the eighteenth century.

If Mannerism was the prevailing movement throughout the last half of the sixteenth century, there was always a strong cross-current. In 1546 Antonio da San Gallo the younger and Giulio Romano both died, and with them died the last vestiges of the High Renaissance associated with Raphael. But did this mean that thereby strict classicism was dead? Palladio[1] about this time stepped to the fore as the great practical exponent in Venetia of Vitruvius's

---

[1] Palladianism was the firm bridge which bound the Italian Renaissance to the European Renaissance and, as it were, straddled across the Baroque era to merge in the Neo-classicism of the eighteenth century.

doctrines and became the founder of an enduring international school. He was not even a pioneer revivalist, for Serlio of a previous generation had upheld Vitruvianism as the epitome of architectural standards, to deviate from which he termed "sinning". Moreover Serlio had been the pupil of Peruzzi, who, like Giulio Romano, was a prominent member of the Raphael group. In other words the fundamental rules of the Ancients were never entirely overlooked in Italy even during the most Mannerist decades of the sixteenth century.

What distinguishes Mannerist buildings from Renaissance buildings is, especially, a flagrant disregard of the rules of the Ancients— which are comprised in the Five Orders. I do not mean to imply that those sixteenth-century hybrid European styles, such as the Plateresque in Spain, the so-called "Flemish" in the Low Countries and Northern Germany, the François Premier in France, the Elizabethan in England, and even the Maltese and the Leccean, were classical, because they made frantic and often pathetic attempts to observe the orders correctly. However manfully the builders in these particular styles struggled to be Vitruvian they were all the while hampered by an inability to throw off a moribund Gothic tradition. Nor do their frequently spirited failures make their buildings Mannerist. In the more distant Mediterranean and northern lands architects were merely ignorant and could not accomplish what they set out to do. The Italian Mannerists on the contrary knew exactly what they were about. Their Mannerism was deliberate. Michelangelo knew perfectly well that he was infringing the rules and he meant thereby to produce masterpieces.

In very truth Mannerist art is highly sophisticated. Its purpose is seldom revealed to the uninitiated. The esoteric learning of Mannerist artists will duly explain what at first may strike us as incomprehensible in their works. Thus the horns upon the forehead of Michelangelo's Moses derive from Exodus XXXIV, v. 29, wherein Moses's face, after the prophet came down from Mount Sinai, is described as reflecting the divine glory. The Hebrew verb, *gâran*, meaning "to shine forth", derives from *géren*, a "horn". Hence the literal translation of the Vulgate, known to Michelangelo, runs: *cornuta esset facies*

—"his face was horned". The strangely bold façade of the Palazzo degli Omenoni in Milan is distinguished by eight immense captives crouching under the weight of the superstructure. Upon each of these carved figures—they are evidently Persians—is inscribed the name of the tribe he is meant to represent, Parthus, Sarmula, Adiabenus and so on. The precise order in which these tribes were subdued was thought significant by Leone Leoni, who designed and built the palace.

And now arises a further complication which should be a salutary warning to an art historian against becoming too specific. I have instanced Giulio Romano as belonging to the Raphael school. Yet Romano was responsible for one of the earliest of all absolutely Mannerist buildings, namely the Palazzo del Tè in Mantua. The palace was begun in 1526 and finished in 1534. To make its extraordinarily unconventional elevations conform to the theory that Mannerism was the direct outcome of the disaster to the Papacy it is tempting to hazard that the building's style changed after the news of the sack of Rome had reached Romano's ears. But such speculation is clearly absurd. The new style is certainly an abrupt departure from that of buildings in Rome like the Villa Madama and the Palazzo Lante of the second decade of the century. Then the swing of serene proportions was still the order of the day in architecture. In the Palazzo del Tè the elevations are broken by unequally spaced bays; window and door pediments dissolve into the wall surface instead of being kept distinct features supported by columns or jambs. And the strangest liberties are taken in a slipping of triglyphs from the entablature as though they had been dislocated by an earthquake and the introduction of uneven blocks of masonry among the rustication.[1] Sanmicheli also built in the 1530s in a somewhat similar manner. His Palazzo Bevilacqua in Verona, with its calculated irregularities and lack of rhythm, is quite unlike what this orthodox classicist had produced at Orvieto and Montefiascone in the Papal

---

[1] An extreme example of Mannerist contrariness is the six horses painted by Romano in the Sala dei Cavalli. These life-size thoroughbreds are made to stand upon narrow entablatures in quite unrealistic openings.

States, or what he was to produce again in Venice twenty years later. And Sansovino in his arresting Zecca in Venice (5) built what at first sight may seem a Roman palace by Raphael, but in reality departs in several essentials from High Renaissance proprieties. The window surrounds of his *piano nobile* are pushed forward as far as the centre of the ringed wall columns, and their duplicated lintels project beyond the circumference of the columns.

It almost seems as if there was something in the air of northern Italy that affected artists, who, having submitted in Rome to a strict classical training, threw off the shackles as soon as they reached freedom from the seat of old learning. I have already remarked how in Tuscany Beccafumi's and Pontormo's painting reacted from the High Renaissance during the second decade. The truth is that once away from Raphael's powerful personality artists fell under the influence of one still stronger. With Raphael's death in 1520 the spirit that had infused a serenity into artistic composition evaporated. His disciples felt free to go their own ways and political circumstances soon compelled those who had not already left to disperse from Rome. The classical rule once relaxed, the disciples allowed themselves to be tossed about by the *Zeitgeist*.

The *Zeitgeist*, quite apart from Wölfflin's natural exhaustion of the logical perfection expressed by the Renaissance, was the almost indefinable outcome of political and religious tension in Christendom, a tension first felt in the north of the peninsula which was furthest from the political hegemony of Rome and so in the van to urge reform. If this unease was reflected in the arts before Michelangelo expressed it, his art, slow to develop and titanic as befitted his temperament, came to epitomize it. In certain respects a comparison of the great artist with Byron, likewise the *enfant terrible* of a later European upheaval, is not irrelevant. The temperaments of the two men were very similar. Wayward and mercurial, deeply brooding, quick to anger and infinitely fertile, both reacted passionately to disturbances not of their making. But neither was fundamentally in harmony with the discontent to which he lent his sympathy. Both were too conscious of their birth to be wholehearted rebels. Here is the sardonic truth. Byron remained the incorrigible aristocrat although he became the prophet of doom to the monarchy which was the source of his indispensable nobility. Michelangelo retained his unshakeable faith in the Catholic Church, to which he owed not only his chief patronage but his spiritual exaltation, in spite of his thunder against papal abuses. The romantic genius of the two men captured the public imagination of their times and influenced their lesser followers sometimes to a risible degree.

Michelangelo's youth and early manhood were passed before a background of continuous political uncertainty in Florence. Invasion by the French, the shiftiness, treachery and expulsion of the Medici, the fanatical theocracy of Savonarola and the reinstatement of the Medici followed in rapid succession. Michelangelo found himself torn by conflicting loyalties to the Medici, to whom he was largely indebted for his own upbringing and learning and for his father's exiguous honours, and to the Republic of Florence which claimed his patriotism and love. To add fuel to this conflict there was his love-hate for his father and spendthrift brethren. Adrian Stokes[1] reveals Michelangelo's extraordinary son–wife relationship with his hopeless old father which contributed to the contradictory passivity of his otherwise forceful character and the consequent "tension of his forms" in art. To this cause we may even trace his peculiar brand of homosexuality and its influence upon the course of Mannerism. Vexations and divided loyalties pursued him well into middle life. His father, ever complaining and making demands upon him, lived to a great age. Successive Medici princes and popes first patronized and then thwarted him. Owing to their attentions he was unable to avoid playing a prominent part in the political fortunes of his native state, and was obliged to adopt the rôle of military engineer in the sacks and sieges which beset Florence. These external events inevitably interrupted his art, and a to-and-fro favour and disgrace with reigning authorities were the cause of alternating exhilarations and frustrations, of which the effects upon his output were immeasurable.

[1] Adrian Stokes, *Michelangelo,* 1955.

Wölfflin, before the term Mannerism had in fact been coined, held Michelangelo directly responsible for that disruptive element in the arts which preceded the age of the Baroque.[1] He condemned the works of his later years, the Medici Chapel, the Last Judgement, the Florentine Pietà and the frescoes—the Conversion of St. Paul and the Crucifixion of St. Peter—in the Capella Paolina at the Vatican, for their renunciation of every contact with nature and the influence they had upon the consequent formalization of art. Raphael being now out of the way Michelangelo reigned supreme. His fame during his lifetime was indeed tremendous. We have only to recall some of the things contemporaries did to, and said of, him. Recognizing the dawn of his superior genius Torregiani in a fit of jealousy broke his nose while they were pupils together in the Medicean Academy, a mark of esteem which remained with him all his life. Vasari, who knew and revered him deeply, wrote: "the Ruler of heaven was pleased to turn the eyes of his clemency towards earth, and perceiving the fruitlessness of so many labours . . . he resolved . . . to send the world a spirit endowed with universality of power in each art . . .", and so forth in a strain that could hardly be more laudatory. Nor were these words sycophantic, for by the time they were written the object of them was dead. Don Francesco de Medici, a prince of the Royal House, admired him so unstintedly that he always spoke uncovered in his presence. Leo X said to him, "You frighten everyone, even Popes". And we know how Julius II, who it is true treated him with parsimony and often with high-handed disdain, nevertheless had not the patience to wait for the dust in the Sistine Chapel to subside, on the removal of the scaffolding, so anxious was he to inspect the finished ceiling.

A vast number of Michelangelo's admirers and imitators failed to discern the deep and turbulent disquiet that underlay his creations. They may have appreciated the surface symbolism which he had invented. Not only throughout Italy, but in France as well, they readily adopted, for example, his figure in a swirling cloak as an image of God the Father. For several centuries they copied the poses

---

[1] H. Wölfflin, *Die Klassische Kunst*, 1899.

and expressions of his slaves and sybils upon vaults and above windows. But they were incapable of understanding the *ansia Michelangiolesca*, the *terribilità* behind his gigantic creations. It was rather the quirks and conceits of his style which appealed to their limited understanding. As happens in periods of transition from one order of society to another, the search for a particular mould of elegance in which to imprison a new concept of formal beauty resulted in strange experiments and affectations. Whereas the poetasters of the second quarter of the nineteenth century wore open-necked shirts and assumed injured airs of being misunderstood, the painter Rosso at night time disinterred corpses from cemeteries to draw them in a state of decomposition, and Parmigianino died worn out from abortive experiments at alchemy and magic. The extravagances of these Michelangelesque painters were just as harmless as those of the early Victorian devotees of Byron, only perhaps bolder as suited their higher stature.

When at the beginning of his career Michelangelo quickly became one of the great artists of the High Renaissance it was in the rank of sculptor first and painter secondly. He never built in the High Renaissance style, and his architecture coincided with the Counter-reformation. He devoted the greater part of his time to architecture in the last years of his life only, and not until 1547 did he become Architect-in-Chief to St. Peter's. The decade saw the opening of the Council of Trent in which Michelangelo played a considerable part behind the scenes. It also witnessed the development of his profound religious preoccupations and his reluctant belief in that inexorable, jealous God whom he envisaged in the Last Judgement. This stage was followed by alternate doubts and protestations of faith induced by Platonic reasoning and keen sorrows for his past sins, which he expressed in the Sonnets of his old age. Henceforth this man of Olympian moods lived the life of an ascetic, eating sparingly of bread and wine and sleeping little. He abased himself before God, and was to be found nursing his old servant Urbino or lying in his clothes night after night beside him on the deathbed, the peasant Urbino whom he had previously made rich in the anticipation that he would survive his master. But Michelangelo could not entirely dissociate himself from affairs of this world. He allied himself to that wise group of humanists who looked for certain compromises with the German malcontents and recognized the high desirability of Church reforms while yet remaining loyal to the papacy. Cardinals Gasparo Contarini, Jacopo Sadoleto and Reginald Pole inside the Church were the advocates of the moderate party which Vittoria Colonna, the Egeria of Michelangelo's later life, warmly supported. But the efforts of the progressives were regarded with suspicion in Rome and failed.

Michelangelo's earliest building ventures, the Medici Chapel and the Biblioteca Laurenziana at S. Lorenzo, Florence (7), were planned and begun in the late 1520s when he was in his mid-fifties. These first essays were subject to interruptions owing to political events and we do not know how far they had progressed when in 1534 their creator left Florence for ever.

In the famous vestibule to the Biblioteca (7) the absolute departure from accepted classical canons of architecture is well exemplified. Michelangelo has, as Pevsner points out, deliberately reversed the usual situation by recessing his coupled wall columns and projecting the intermediate panels. The brackets, which presumably are meant to support the columns, are so far advanced on plinths, themselves exaggerated in depth, that they can do nothing of the sort and anyway are far too flimsy. The tabernacle frames in the wall spaces have pilasters which narrow at the bottom and are crowned by insecure, pinched capitals. In fact we have something profoundly revolutionary, yet with a beauty all its own. The staircase of curved treads and broken flights with scroll supports is the ancestor of all Baroque stairs in the world. For what is contemplated here is "movement"—a new concept—within a restricted space by means of reversed functions of architectural members. Michelangelo in his architecture has tried to release some caged force, just as in his sculpture he maintained that the statue pre-existed in the block of marble and was merely waiting to be freed and Ariel-like come to life. Indeed we can see those half-executed figures (3) for Julius II's tomb (now in the Accademia, Florence) in the very act of emerging from captivity. Young Nicholas Stone seemed to understand something of what Michelangelo was striving after in the Biblioteca Laurenziana when he noted in his diary of 1638 that: "No one can imagine how graceful these stairs do look (by any description) in the reality; being (as I said at first) for so much the rarest studied things than one can likely see."

For a still more startling contrast between the Classical and Mannerist treatment of architecture there is Antonio da San Gallo the younger's Palazzo Farnese in Rome, to which after the architect's death in 1546 Michelangelo has added a top storey. Here he makes window heads break through the entablature—to become a favourite piece of Mannerist daredevilry—and supports them upon tenuous consoles, which give a singularly top-heavy effect. In the courtyard upper stage his window-heads are made to rest on brackets which descend into *guttae*, quite detached from the surrounds (*6*). Were it not that the material Michelangelo used was precisely the same travertine and that little lapse of time was allowed between the two works, his treatment of the palace would in contrast with San Gallo's suave classicism appear outrageous. And it must be confessed that in this particular context Michelangelo's eccentricities seem hardly justified.

At the time of his death Michelangelo's plans and designs for the Piazza del Campidoglio were well under way (*8*). But he never finished the work, which with certain breaks was continued right into the seventeenth century. This alone is proof how well Michelangelo's Mannerism was respected by his Baroque successors. His every conceived detail was carried out down to the pavement made oval and slightly raised in the centre—where Marcus Aurelius was placed on his plinth—in order to withdraw attention from the trapezoidal shape of the area, as well as the perimeter of two recessed steps.

In allowing that Michelangelo's genius was the ultimate impetus of the Mannerist movement we remember that he was not the founder of a school of architecture. He himself realized this and never spoke a truer phrase than when he exclaimed, "My architecture is destined to produce some great fools!" In his architecture, as in his painting, he had plenty of imitators rather than disciples; in fact he had imitators centuries after Mannerism had become a spectral fashion of the past. In all the branches of the arts which he practised he was a solitary. What ordinary man of talent could be expected fully to apprehend that titanic mind? Did Michelangelo truly know himself? He was like someone who, seeking to penetrate the absolute mysteries, peers into the depths of a pool and sees nothing but the reflection of his own tormented features. It is doubtful whether any artist more than dimly divined what Michelangelo was aiming at before Bernini and Borromini appeared in the following century. And of them the one grasped the implication of his sculpture and the other of his architecture.

Giacomo del Duca (1520–1601), a Sicilian, the pupil who worked in closest contact with Michelangelo and helped towards the completion of the two palaces facing each other on the Campidoglio, vicariously fulfilled the spirit of his architecture. Del Duca, like his master, was primarily a sculptor. But he is chiefly remembered for the little church of S. Maria in Trivio close to the Trevi Fountain, which he rebuilt, and the cupola of S. Maria di Loreto by Trajan's Forum. S. Maria in Trivio has a distinctive façade in that loose rhythm which found many an echo in the northern countries during the seventeenth century. The central door with its curious ears and scrolled sides was copied and reproduced in Commonwealth England by Balthazar Gerbier and his practically anonymous school of provincial builders. The cupola of S. Maria di Loreto, rather too big for San Gallo's dome, has nevertheless an original and engaging outline of surrounding shafts like a cluster of giant candles on a birthday cake.

6   *Palazzo Farnese, Rome (after 1546):*
Courtyard window
Michelangelo, architect

7   *Biblioteca   Laurenziana,   Florence:*
Entrance from Vestibule (c. 1530)
Michelangelo, architect

8 *Palazzo dei Conservatori, Campidoglio, Rome*
Michelangelo (1474–1563), architect

9 *Villa di Papa Giulio, Rome (begun 1551)*
Vignola, architect

10   *Palazzo Cambiaso, Genoa: the Entrance*
Galeazzo Alessi (1512–72), architect

11   *The University, Genoa: Steps to the Courtyard*
Bartolomeo Bianco (d. 1657), architect

12 *S. Fidele, Milan (1569)*
Pellegrino Tibaldi, architect

ALESSI (1512–72) AND TIBALDI (1527–97)

There are two architects of del Duca's generation, both better known than he, who were profoundly affected by what they considered to be the modern fashion of building evolved by Michelangelo. They were Galeazzo Alessi, del Duca's senior by eight years, and Pellegrino Tibaldi, his junior by seven. Both came from the north of Italy. The one is chiefly associated with Genoa, the other with Milan. The architecture of both falls within the Mannerist period, although that of the younger man (Tibaldi lived until 1597) came near to over-lapping the Baroque age.

Alessi, who was a native of Perugia, formed his style when very young on an intensive study of Michelangelo's works in Rome. He imbibed from him a notably masculine and monumental manner. His is truly the architecture of revolt against the femininism of Raphael. He developed a new style to satisfy new requirements, which in Genoa meant above all an outlet for the vast fortunes then being acquired by the plutocracy of this wealthy republic. Grandiose palaces were demanded by a powerful commercial nobility who desired them to be ostentatious, as befitted their resources, and original in order to proclaim the new dynasties they were establishing. It was the Sauli family who in 1548 called Alessi to Genoa, where for seventeen years he remained without a break and where after only one short absence he returned.

Alessi determined the conception of the Genoese town palace, which became the most magnificent in Europe, with its great central hall or court, and of the suburban villa, without a court but with a garden closely related to the building. His façades are usually of two unbroken orders of pilasters over a massive rusticated basement. They have very well developed and richly carved cornices. Alessi was particularly careful with his ornament, which was sparing but bold; and of his great church S. Maria-in-Carignano in Genoa he wrote with evident satisfaction that "the decoration is apportioned according to the manner of the ancients in their temples". The façades of his villas are characterized by slightly projecting ends and tightly assembled central windows. Balustrades punctuated with great balls are a usual crowning feature. He was fond of breaking his inside walls with large niches. He laid out what is still one of the most splendid streets of palaces in the world, the Strada Nuova or, as it was termed in its heyday, the Strada Aurea, to which he contributed several palaces, notably the Cambiaso (*10*) and Lercari; for as well as being an architect he was one of the earliest town planners. John Evelyn, who saw the Strada Nuova in the 1640s, thought it superior to any street on the Continent. Its prestige in northern Europe is well known. Rubens in his book *I Palazzi di Genova*, which incidentally had a wide circulation in England, took the majority of his plates from palaces in the Strada Nuova: in fact Evelyn believed that Rubens had designed the street. Roger Pratt, the first professional architect in England, studied the palaces on the spot, and the development of his Coleshill House of two stages under wide eaves and with central windows huddled together was an obvious consequence. It is no exaggeration to state that the rectangular English country house of the last half of the seventeenth century, too commonly known as the "Wren" type, was derived through Pratt and Rubens from Alessi in the first instance, although in the course of transformation it naturally became much modified.

In Genoa the building of vast palaces in the Alessi tradition was continued long after Mannerism had been forgotten in Rome. Bartolomeo Bianco, official architect to the Republic, carried on the tradition until his death in 1657. This important architect had a strong dramatic sense. He understood the problem of balancing and fusing great masses, such as the lofty centre block of the Palazzo Durazzo-Pallavicini flanked by loggias of three stages and open arcades above, and developed a keen sense of perspective effects, such as the vista through the courtyard of the Palazzo Balbi Senarega towards the garden and grotto of giants, and the lion steps up to the courtyard of the University (*11*). He, even more than Alessi, took advantage of this steep hilly town in planning his palaces on different levels. They have a quality of eternal strength. The façades are severe and naked, usually constructed on a huge podium. The entrances are imposing, the cornices deep and ornaments extremely sparse. Bianco cannot, however, be termed a Baroque architect, and his elevations present something of the impregnable aspect of Florentine palaces of the early Renaissance.

Tibaldi, who came from Bologna, spent most of his working life and died in Milan. Like Alessi he was held in high esteem and heaped with honours. In 1547–50 he was in Rome, where he began his career as a painter of large-scale frescoes under the massive influence of Michelangelo. About the year 1562 he moved from Bologna to Milan under the patronage of St. Charles Borromeo. His paintings are often architectural. His *Decollazione di S. Giovanni* (Beheading of St. John) in the Brera is enacted before a church of which the curved colonnade and steps are thoroughly Baroque. In fact certain of Tibaldi's later buildings appear more Baroque than Mannerist. A flowing line throughout the composition, without any of the bizarreness of the early seventeenth-century Roman church façades, distinguishes S. Sebastiano, Milan, built in 1577. This remarkable building with its rotunda and high drum to the dome and its circular, becupola'd sanctuary almost anticipates the swelling contours of the famous Salute in Venice. One is tempted to ask whether Tibaldi found a hint for his lovely dome, with its vast attendant scrolls, in Raphael's background temple of the *Spozalizio* painting now in the Brera. To contrast S. Sebastiano with the church of S. Fidele (*12*), which he began for the Jesuits eight years previously, is enlightening. There the rich pre-Vignolan front is broken into separate jerky units, with self-sufficient tabernacles for statues between the engaged columns, and is still absolutely Mannerist.

In 1587 Tibaldi abandoned Milan and moved to the Escorial near Madrid. He spent many years decorating the Library ceiling in a manner reminiscent of both the Sistine Chapel and the Vatican Loggie, and was rewarded by King Philip II with a marquisate. But with so many churches and palaces to his credit in Milan and the north of Italy he may be considered the founder of a new Lombardic style of architecture, which he had first evolved through long experiment on canvas and in fresco and accordingly invested

43

with a massive looseness and suppleness of perspective associated with painting rather than building.

VIGNOLA (1507–73)

Even more famous in his day than Alessi and Tibaldi and of great importance in the continuity of Roman architecture was Jacopo Barozzi, commonly known as Vignola. Older than Alessi by five years he survived him by one, dying in 1573. Vignola was unusual in being exclusively an architect. Of very high principles, unassuming and thorough, he is remarkable for the extreme precision of his detailed units. His architecture is logical, even cold. The wide reputation he earned in his lifetime is not so much justified by what he achieved— for most of his buildings were planned in collaboration with others —as by the standards he set and the precedents he established in consequence of deep meditation upon the nature of his art. The Villa di Papa Giulio (*9*), built in association with Ammanati, and the Gesù, actually finished by Della Porta and others, became archetypes, the one of the post-Renaissance country villa and garden, the other of church architecture, both of which traditions survived well into the eighteenth century and were followed throughout Christendom with almost relentless piety.

The importance of Vignola is that, although he flourished during the high tide of Mannerism, his ultimate insistence upon classical forms created a bridgehead between the Renaissance and the Baroque. His *Regola delli Cinque Ordini* proves this point. But it did not, like Palladio's book, preach an undiluted Vitruvianism. It became a text-book of absolute authority at a time when more literature on art appeared than ever before or since until the present century. To some extent he may claim to have saved the Renaissance from subsiding into chaos. His work at the Villa Giulio, begun in 1551, shows a turning away from his Mannerist upbringing in Italy and also in France at the Court of Francis I. Here we find evidence of "a new personal classicism based on antiquity" evolving under our eyes. The earlier, entrance façade, with its closely packed central

44

feature and disparate upper windows with conceited little crests, is
markedly different from the later, garden façade, where the old
classical triumphal arch motif is intro-
duced, although on a curve. There is a
great contrast between Vignola's re-
introduction of classical forms on this
front of the casino and Ammanati's tight
sequence of buildings and walled vistas
which confine the garden. Ammanati remained a thorough Mannerist, and his
contribution to the villa, a masterpiece of
garden layout of this epoch, is the exact
reverse of what was to come in the late
seventeenth and the eighteenth centuries.
His conception of a garden is thoroughly
introvert, suburban if you like (*13*). Instead of reaching into the wild country
it confines tamed nature within the bounds
of genteel artificiality. Surprise after surprise is encountered within a small compass
as hemi-cycles and nymphaeums reveal
themselves as though designed expressly for
evening parties and theatricals (*16*). At

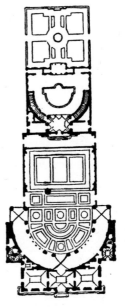

13   *Villa Giulio,
Rome*

Frascati and Tivoli, a little further away from the City's centre, we
see within the next fifty years similar enchanting paradises arise on a
rather more splendid scale owing maybe to the advantage offered in
each case by the steep terrain. Casinos and statuary, grottos, jets
and cascades, remained the rage for a century and a half until they
were all swept away in favour of the long pleached vistas of the Le
Nôtre school.

In church design Vignola's originality is most apparent. During
the High Renaissance a church was an entity. All its features were
considered parts of a whole artistic conception. In Bramante's
Tempietto of S. Pietro in Montorio, for example, it is inconceivable
to consider the dome by itself. The very junctions of the lead panels

have been devised so as to fall into place over the pilasters of the drum and they in their turn over the columns of the peristyle of the temple. Your eye takes in either the entire building or nothing at all. During the Mannerist period, on the contrary, the separate parts of a church are self-sufficient. The beautiful domes of S. Andrea della Valle and S. Carlo in Corso cannot be seen in relation to the façades of these churches and were never meant to be, even when constructed. If at Tibaldi's S. Fidele, Milan, you were able to suppress the four tabernacle frames within the outer bays, the cartouches and reliefs within the inner bays and the lesser orders within the larger orders, you would still be left with a building no less recognizable as a respectable church than it is at present. For the design of the whole would not suffer. It might even improve. Mr. John Coolidge has expressed this sentiment in extreme terms: "If the typical High Renaissance edifice had been a hierarchy of forms, the late Renaissance was apt to be a mere federation, and a federation that sometimes verged on chaos."[1] Vignola realized this prevailing tendency of his age and he set about to reconsider the design of a church, not again as a whole (the men of the Baroque age were to do that) but as a study of juxtapositions and contrasts. For St. Peter's, where he succeeded Michelangelo as chief architect, he designed two subsidiary domes, not intended by his predecessor, to form deliberate contrasts to their surroundings. They were not executed; but Etienne Du Pérac's drawings of 1568 clearly show what was in his mind. At the same time he attempted to return to a simplification of surface pattern by concentrating upon a strictly correct use of the orders, and by making the plan felt throughout the composition. The little oratory of S. Andrea in Via Flaminia and S. Anna dei Palafrenieri, begun the year of his death, are the first churches to be built on an elliptical plan and to suggest the emphatic new plasticity which was his aim.

Vignola's avowed attempts at correlating surface units may not at first be apparent at the Gesù which is always associated with his name. The façade of this famous church (*17*), the progenitor of

[1] John Coolidge, *Vignola*, etc. *Marsyas II*, 1942.

how many familiar offspring throughout Europe known indeed as
"Vignolan façades", is, however, not to Vignola's design. He died
before it could be begun and when the interior of the church had
only reached the cornice. Della Porta altered the
original design of the elevation but adhered to the
principle which Vignola had set, if not quite to the
letter.

The church of which the nave was started in
1568 was the first on a grand scale to be built
for the Society of Jesus. It is not surprising that
Vignola, who had built for the Farnese family
at Piacenza and Caprarola, was chosen as
architect by the rich and powerful Cardinal
Alessandro Farnese, who bore all expenses of
the undertaking. Before this date Jesuit churches
were austere and sombre as befitted the spartan militancy and mysticism of the Society's

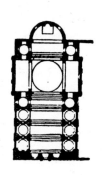

14 *Church of
the Gesù,
Rome*

early years. Furthermore we must bear in mind that the lavish
decoration of the Gesù belongs not to the sixteenth century but to the
next. During the first hundred years of its existence the church was
not very splendid, nor even what we now like to think essentially
Jesuit. The great painted ceiling by G. B. Gaulli, splashing over its
frame down to window level, was not finished until 1683, and the
surge of stucco relief with which Antonio Raggi and others had
encased the windows a few years before was part of Gaulli's scheme.
The Loyola Chapel, which by virtue of its ambitious altar of rare
marbles and lapis lazuli conveys the impression of great opulence,
was added by Andrea Pozzo between 1685 and 1699. Sixteenth-
century Jesuit churches, of which the Gesù was the epitome, were
almost deprived of interior decoration. It is Vignola's plan of the
church which is the novelty. To be more exact it is a revival inspired
by the fifteenth-century Alberti's plan of S. Andrea at Mantua, thus
affording another example of Vignola's fruitful investigation of the
purest and most primitive classical examples. At any rate the
basilican plan of the Gesù was followed almost unvaryingly in Rome

until about 1630[1] and elsewhere in Europe until the eighteenth century.

Generally speaking, the Renaissance had preferred the central to the Latin cross plan for churches, so that the whole vastness of an interior might be appreciated on entry. The Baroque was to return to this preference. The Jesuits, however, for practical reasons did not favour it. Unlike the ancient monastic orders, they dispensed with choral offices. Instead, services were to be shared with the congregation. Hence the elimination from their churches of the usual screen, thus affording an uninterrupted view of the high altar. This was their main objective, which was confirmed by Vignola's provision of an unusually shallow apse, of truncated transepts and a dome over a wide crossing to shed a flood of light upon the sanctuary. It was Cardinal Farnese who, with an eye upon his purse, insisted on the single nave with simple series of chapels along either side and the barrel vault—both of which happened to lend themselves admirably to the exuberant process of Baroque decoration over a hundred years later. In this way the famous archetype of Jesuit churches was derived from a combination of tradition, liturgical innovation, good sense, economy and chance.

All, therefore, the Counter-reformation Jesuits dictated to the architect for his elaboration was the bare plan of the Gesù.[2] The hall church domed was not then entirely a Jesuit invention. Strzygowski[3] saw in it a reversion to those Armenian churches with long naves and truncated transepts which reached their highest development in the seventh century. Now Italy, it is true, always had close commercial ties with the countries of the Near East, and Jesuit missions were from the first scattered over the face of Asia Minor. But whereas the dome of the Church of the Apostles

[1] Exceptions to the Gesù plan formula are D. Fontana's and F. Ponzio's Greek cross chapels in S. Maria Maggiore and S. Carlo ai Catinari respectively.

[2] Actually the dome is Della Porta's but it follows the Vignolan principle as regards setting. It was the forerunner of a series of Roman Baroque cupolas, most of which excelled it. For it is an uncomfortable, squat little affair lacking nobility.

[3] J. Strzygowski, *Origin of Christian Church Art*, 1923.

at Ani (sixth century) and that of the church at Thalish (A.D. 668)
were set centrally—a situation
followed by the Renaissance in its
centralized churches and advocated
by Leonardo and Bramante—
Vignola ordained that his should
be nearer the apse than the middle
of the nave, where indeed the crossing of Gothic churches is usually
to be found. Furthermore the
Armenians had designed their
churches to be viewed as structural
masses from all sides. Vignola on
the contrary followed the Renaissance method of concentrating
attention upon the façade almost
exclusively.

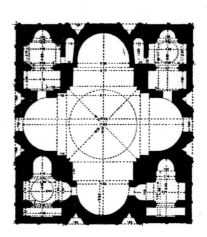

15 *Ani: Church of the Apostles*

The no-less renowned façade of the Gesù in two stages of five bays
in the lower and three in the upper under a pediment, had likewise
been outlined by Alberti—in S. Maria Novella at Florence between
1456 and 1470. Alberti's upper stage, for which there was no precedent in classical times, was merely the width of the pre-existing
Gothic nave bound to the lower stage by large scrolls meant to
hide the roofs of the aisles or side chapels. Della Porta at the Gesù
modified Vignola's original Albertian design. He accentuated the
height of the façade by diminishing the importance of the side
wings and concentrating his detail upon the centre. Even so his
façade has a spreading effect like a hen brooding and fluffing out
her wing feathers. Della Porta's most notable change was the
introduction of a triangular within a semicircular pediment over
the main door, a conceit taken from Michelangelo's Laurenziana,
which the purist Vignola would not have countenanced for a moment.
In spite of this single departure from strict orthodoxy the resulting
façade—so soon to be repeated all over Europe—is a decent, if
sophisticated, tight-laced composition that has neither the monodic

simplicity of the fifteenth century nor the thematic rhythm of the seventeenth. In other words it is not an object of startling beauty and becomes frankly boring with repetition.

THE LATE COUNTER-REFORMATION

Giacomo Della Porta, who was Vignola's pupil and follower, was only thirty-three when called upon to complete the Gesù on his master's death. Without the dignity of Vignola or the strength of Michelangelo, he was an architect of extraordinary fecundity who evolved new forms. His façade of the Madonna dei Monti, Rome, was a modification of that of the Gesù, simpler, less fussy and more pleasing. It is vertical rather than horizontal and has in all five bays between pilasters. The niches flanking the single door and window provide just the right punctuation to a plain and dignified front which had an immense influence upon the Baroque architects. Della Porta made his S. Anastasia with twin square lateral towers the first of another popular type of Roman church front. Although the façade was altered in the 1630s the towers remain.

Della Porta's working life coincided with the late Counter-reformation under the pontificate of Sixtus V (1585–90). It was not a period of much original development of the arts. The worst fears of the Church were now over. The Council of Trent had determined the course of things to come. The conscious piety of Popes and prelates and the general austerity of living could be mitigated a little. Rome regained some of its natural gaiety. A visitor to the City in 1581 was able to write: "Rome occupies now a middle place between licentiousness and strict morality, and everyone is all the better for it." Even the severe St. Charles Borromeo, commenting approvingly upon the public display of well-being, was heard to remark: "Love God and keep a carriage", so great was the number of carriages in the streets. The prevailing complacency was reflected in useful but prosaic architecture. Sixtus was an ambitious, determined man who within a short luster brought many benefits to Rome. He laid on the Acqua Felice, thus bringing the first water system of modern times over the Campagna to the Seven Hills. He personally devised and saw carried out a network of five straight streets across the heart of the City, and so became the first Roman town planner since the Augustan era. He raised the vast obelisk before St. Peter's, and the citizens of Rome celebrated with a *fiesta*. He then set up four others, and in the following century elegant squares were fashioned around them. He had the great cathedral cupola completed to Michelangelo's original design by Della Porta and Domenico Fontana within twenty-two months. During his reign Fontana built the Lateran Palace, the Quirinal Palace and a new wing to the Vatican.

Yet Sixtus V was not a man of taste. He had no regard for the Roman monuments, which he treated simply as quarries for his own undertakings; and he wanted to turn the Colosseum into a factory. The claim that the Baroque age was launched by Sixtus is unfounded. Domenico Fontana, his hard-worked instrument, willingly subordinated his talents to the overweening projects of his master. He told the Pope: "No one can better carry out a plan than the man who has conceived it, for no one can perfectly interpret the thoughts of another." Unfortunately Fontana was a dull, unimaginative architect whom no rewards—he was made a knight, then a nobleman and presented with gold chains and ten prebends yielding a fortune—could enliven. His vast palaces are stretches of unrelieved tedium. His Cappella Sistina in S. Maria Maggiore, in spite of the polychrome wealth of its materials upon which numerous artists were set to manufacture lifeless Michelangelesque statuary, is typical of the late Counter-reformation.

Such was the state of Roman art until the first decade of the next century. The movement to which the magic name of Michelangelo is lent as chief exponent, but of which he was not the originator, did not produce a great output. Michelangelo's influence upon the sixteenth century was hardly beneficial or even fertile. Painting suffered in the same way as architecture and sculpture. It is of course a commonplace that the reigning generation despises its immediate predecessors. But there is frequent testimony that the seventeenth century was unusually critical of those generations which preceded it on account of their artificialities and affectations. I have already said that it referred to their style as "Manierismo". Baldinucci[1] wrote of their *pittura ammanierata* and their *decadenza*; Passeri[2] that painting in the hands of these *torbidi cervelli* all but fell into the abyss from which there is no exit; and Baglione[3] that, whereas painting was born with Raphael and Michelangelo and revived by the Caracci, in between it became languid and downcast. We do not have to interpret these assertions by the standards of High Baroque art, for the seventeenth century was still too close to understand or sympathize with the underlying causes of its predecessors' style which we are able to see in truer perspective. But the consensus of several eminent art historians of the seventeenth century is not without some significance.

[1] F. Baldinucci, *Vita del Cav. Gio. Lorenzo Bernini*, 1682.
[2] G. B. Passeri, *Vite de' Pittori, scultori ed architetti . . . in Roma dal 1641–1673*, published 1772.
[3] G. Baglione, *Vite de' Pittori, scultori et architetti*, 1642.

16 *Villa di Papa Giulio, Rome:
Nymphaeum (c. 1550–60)
Bartolomeo Ammanati, architect*

17 *The Gesù, Rome: façade carried out
(after 1573) by G. della Porta*

18   *"Noli me Tangere", by Correggio (1494–1534)*
(Prado Gallery, Madrid)

2. Baroque

EVERY school of art and architecture, whether western or oriental, Greek or Japanese, moves in a cycle that culminates in the equivalent of a Baroque phase. The Romanesque, the Gothic, even the Neo-classical and Neo-gothic styles—to mention a few within modern times—reached a penultimate florescence of beauty before fading into ultimate extinction. The nineteenth century traced the regular process of growth, maturity and decay in the arts to the state of civilization of the peoples living at the time of each phase of the cycle. They too must be correspondingly adolescent, mature or decadent. Today we can no longer accept this easy theory, and in realizing that a uniform pattern of civilization does not invariably coincide with the evolution of a school of art we look for more particular explanations of each phase as it comes about.

The attempts by eminent scholars to define the Baroque movement which followed the European Renaissance have been so numerous and conflicting that not without some temerity I risk a further confusion of the subject. It is not unlike trying to determine the exact colour of a material in different lights. The Baroque will look different under the rays of different moods. One scholar has said that it is a break-away from the tyranny of the antique[1]; another that it comes from the Germanic north which has never been Classical and so is opposed to the Classical concept[2]; one that the term Baroque art is a contradiction, for the dominant desire of the Baroque is to stupefy, and true art never does this[3]; another

---

[1] Geoffrey Webb, *Baroque Art*, 1947.
[2] H. Wölfflin, *Die Klassische Kunst*, 1899.
[3] B. Croce, *Storia dell'età barocca in Italia*, 1925.

that Baroque art is subject to the strictest laws of composition, and its purpose is exact.[1] Often too the same authority will contradict himself. Eugenio D'Ors in a book of brilliant paradoxes refers to the conflicting intentions of the Baroque as displayed in a single gesture.[2] The Baroque, he says, does not know what it wants. He takes as an example Correggio's famous picture *Noli me Tangere*, wherein Christ, who is clearly meant to reassure the Magdalen, is depicted as repelling her (*18*). She who is repentant is made to look wanton; in order to follow him she squats on her heels. Later, however, d'Ors clearly states that the character of the Baroque is quite normal. Somerset Maugham makes a similar complaint to d'Ors's first when he writes that El Greco is ready to sacrifice truth of gesture to beauty of attitude.[3] The Baroque has been called the essentially patrician art, exclusive to an unhealthy, artificial aristocracy.[4] Frank Granger has termed it the art of the people, signifying a joyousness of free expression, the word deriving from the mediaeval Latin "baro", meaning a simpleton or the common man, thus the adjective "barocco" implying something which belongs to this ordinary person.[5] We are equally told that in mediaeval Latin the word "barocco" stood for the turgidity of the scholastic reasoning and so became the syllogism which draws conclusions from the absurd. Elsewhere we are assured that the word derives from "barroco", a misshapen pearl which the Portuguese fishermen would discard on the seashore as useless; from the Latin "verruca", meaning a wart; and even from the Arabic "burāg", which is hard earth mixed with stones.[6]

These contradictory definitions do not much matter. What stands to reason is that our word Baroque refers to one historic epoch in western civilization as well as to a particular shape or misshape of

[1] G. Scott, *The Architecture of Humanism*, 1914.
[2] Eugenio D'Ors, *Du Baroque*, 1935.
[3] W. Somerset Maugham, *Don Fernando*, 1935.
[4] M. S. Briggs, *Baroque Architecture*, 1913.
[5] Frank Granger, "A Letter on Baroque": *Times Literary Supplement*, 15 March 1928.
[6] *Chambers's Twentieth Century Dictionary*, under entry "Baroque".

man's mood. As Benedetto Croce rightly says, it had to come. And with the turn of the seventeenth century it came, first to Rome, where it flourished for about a hundred years, even lingering there well into the eighteenth century. By then Italy had ceased to be complete mistress of the arts and the movement was reaching a zenith in Germany and Central Europe. It happened, Croce continues, because humanity wanted it to happen. But when he claims that there was no more cause of it than there is of human sin, he simplifies too much. Admittedly fashions and tastes must change. So does the process of thought. The enquiring mind will welcome the new and spurn the old. Bramante, as Hübner[1] points out, would have been hooted in the streets of Rome in the seventeenth century, just as Borromini would have been lynched in the nineteenth. Indeed a French traveller in the reign of Paul V wrote of Bramante's masterpiece, the Palazzo Giraud: "[It] is not esteemed so much for its structure as for the infinite number of rare and singular treasures which it contains", and Bishop Burnet dismissed a certain Roman palace as "a mean building because it is ancient".[2] Such a condition in itself was sufficiently damning.

The Baroque was, unlike Mannerism, a very purposeful movement. It was, in fact, the first positively novel style to evolve on Roman soil since antiquity. It was, as we shall find from the hands of its greatest artists, a dynamic expression in place of the static harmony and repose of early and full Renaissance art. To that degree only did it break away, not from the tyranny of the antique, but from the Renaissance's complacent interpretation of the antique. It was that interpretation which was outworn. Unlike the Gothic, which had been a complete break in style from the long-decaying Classical ideal of antiquity, the Baroque was rather an inevitable extension of that Classical ideal to whose original source it had returned. It sought to step out into infinity, to exploit the endlessness of space and time instead of confining itself to this earth and concentrating upon the moment. Its creators seemed to defy the limitations of their materials.

[1] A. von Hübner, *Life and Times of Sixtus V*, 1872.
[2] Bishop G. Burnet, *Some Letters . . . in Italy*, 1686.

Sculpture depicted figures in the act of doing rather than contemplating. Architecture by means of optical illusion and by calling
upon the aid of sculpture and painting sought, as Giedion says, to
defy the laws of gravity[1]—certainly to make buildings seem alive.
By the sharp undercutting of carved surfaces, shadows were made
to suggest new plastic dimensions. By the application of chiaroscuro
decoration a pictorial quality, chiefly under the influence of
Caravaggio, was introduced to architecture. Geoffrey Scott associated with the Baroque the word "picturesque", through which
quality, he claimed, it was reconciled to Classicism.[2] In other words
material became "utterly subservient to style". Artists turned away
from matter. Only form counted and the strictest laws of composition. Whether marble, stone, canvas or paint were used they
were made to fulfil, separately or in conjunction, the idea to be expressed.

Gardeners, particularly in France, by means of long vistas per-
petuated the illusion that their landscapes went on for ever. Town
planners were occasionally able to do the same thing. It is what the
seventeenth century delighted in. Bishop Berkeley standing in the
Piazza del Popolo on his first visit to Rome could record "the two
beautiful churches of the same architecture that front the entrance
on either side of the end of the Corso . . . carrying the eye in a straight
line through the middle of the City almost to the Capitol. . . . From
the Guglio [the obelisk] your prospect shoots through these three
streets. All this, I say, is contrived to produce a good effect on the
eye of a newcomer."[3] It was the century of triumphant purpose over
detail. Particulars were subordinated to a grand whole. The arts
were working towards a single end, dominated always by architecture.
The architect emerged as the great co-ordinator. This is why Baroque
sculpture and painting cannot properly be appreciated when detached
from their settings. The architect supervened in every rôle, with his
magic wand of lyricism and light and gaiety. Look at the Potsdam

[1] S. Giedion, *Space, Time and Architecture*, 1954.
[2] Geoffrey Scott, *The Architecture of Humanism*, 1914.
[3] Bishop G. Berkeley, *Journal of a Tour in Italy*, 1717, 1718.

19 *The Laocöon Group (c. 35* B.C.)
(Vatican Galleries)

20 *Marble acroterion of Victory,*
from the Stoa of Zeus, Athens
(late 5th century B.C.)

21 *The Wounded Warrior Pergamese (Archaeological Museum, Venice)*

22 *The Temple of Venus, Baalbec (early 2nd century). An engraving from Robert Wood's Baalbec, 1757*

23 *Arch of Tiberius, Orange* (A.D. *21*)

Palace, where he conjures up a detached screen of columns and entablature, extending apparently aimlessly into the landscape. It was utterly useless, or so no doubt the simple palace gardeners must have thought as they watched it being constructed. But it was essential to the architect's purpose, which was to create an agreeable effect. Architecture was the structure round which the lesser arts revolved or to which they were applied as decoration. The extravagantly pictorial quality of Baroque art is also found in music. The vocal and instrumental compositions of the Venetian Giovanni Gabrieli (1557–1612) were written to be performed sometimes in as many as sixteen parts, of which the antiphonal sounds were often made to issue from different galleries of St. Mark's Cathedral.

"Movement" is of course the key word. And how absurd! As if blocks of stone or paint on a flat surface can move. But it was the Baroque intention notwithstanding. "Movement" is expressed in the everlasting curve made by the Baroque artist, which though used before has never been so played upon as by him, being inseparable from his love of the human form, and above all the female form. *Stil des Werdens*, the style of becoming, the German scholars have called the Baroque to distinguish it from the *Stil des Seins*, the style of being, which is the Renaissance formula. A Baroque work of art is both a work of art and the actual creation of this work, which explains why there is a greater similarity between a sketch and the finished object by Bernini, Rubens or Puget, than between a sketch and finished object by Bramante, Poussin or Le Brun. With the Classical artist the sketch is no more than an idea awaiting completion.

We must, however, beware of supposing that the Baroque was a complete break with the spirit of the immediate past. The Mediaeval tradition persisted in European Catholic countries right into the Baroque centuries, and therefore was deeply infused into the style moulded admittedly from a Classical matrix. The Baroque "combines", to quote Granger, "tradition with experiment", a truism denied by the later Neo-classical generation who failed to recognize that their predecessors had brought to fruition through vivid inspiration and hard thinking a new ideal, whereas they in self-conscious revivalism were labouring to exploit an old one.

BAROQUE IN ANCIENT GREECE AND ROME

The architects of the Italian Baroque returned to the Classical tradition of design which they reproached their predecessors, the Mannerists, for having wilfully misunderstood. With them the correct cult of the antique amounted to a passion. Towards the end of the sixteenth century a rather unhealthy antiquarianism captivated the Romans. It is shown in the spate of views of Augustine ruins which were disseminated for sale all over the City. To some extent this servile archaeological pedantry endured, for we find Innocent X in the middle of the seventeenth century restoring the Piazza Navona to conform exactly to the shape of Domitian's racecourse, which once occupied the site, even at the expense of pulling down the Aldobrandini Palace because it was not aligned to it. But the better side to this exaggerated pietism was that the antique meant the absolute standard by which the merits of a contemporary work of art could be assessed. Furthermore the seventeenth century witnessed an ever increasing exhumation of ancient statuary—most of which in fact was late Roman work or inferior copies of the original Greek—and also the excavation of the foundations of much late Roman architecture. Often these foundations revealed tendencies of a distinctly Baroque kind in their planning.

It is unlikely that the seventeenth-century artists had seen with their own eyes much, if any original Greek sculpture. Certainly they can have seen little Greek architecture to influence their novel methods of building. Yet there is no doubt that in its long, slow evolution Greek art reached a spirited phase analogous if not comparable to Italian Baroque art. It is hardly necessary to state that this so-called "Baroque" phase of Greek art by no means followed the same lines of development as the Italian. But the extremely sensitive idealism, first of Archaic and then of High Classical sculpture, could not continue for ever and had in the course of time to relax. There is undoubtedly some evidence that the rigid and formalized style of Greek architecture relaxed also.

At the end of the fifth century B.C. when the High Classical was nearing exhaustion a difference in Greek sculptural style is noticeable. The famous group of Niobe and her children belongs to this period. Instead of harmonious contemplation the figures exhibit attitudes of intense suffering and wild despair. Niobe's eldest daughter is fleeing before the avenging darts of the invisible Apollo and Artemis while her garments flow behind her in curves. A son crouches, holding the drapery of his right arm over his head as a shield. A marble Victory (*20*) recently excavated in the Stoa of Zeus, Athens, has both legs outstretched, knees bent, body and neck turned and head uplifted. The whole figure, a swirl of clinging and flowing garments deeply undercut, is far more closely related to Bernini's "movement" than to Michelangelo's contemplation.

With the opening of the Hellenistic age about 334 B.C., the year in which Alexander began his conquest of Asia Minor, Greece ceased to be a political and economic entity and declined into part of a vast empire. Henceforth Athens and Hellas produced no more first-class sculpture. Artists moved eastwards. For some three hundred years the Hellenistic age was in the van of history. Repose in sculpture was now quite abandoned in favour of action, or dramatic attitudes, which reached their highest point of technical achievement in the famous Laocöon group (*c.* 35 B.C.) wherein the legendary priest is depicted in an agonized death struggle with serpents (*19*). The culmination of Hellenistic Baroque was in Pergamum. The Pergamese civilization was one of acute anxiety and desperate struggle for existence against the invading Gauls. The days of happy Greek idealism had long since faded into oblivion. Artists sought a passionate realism tinged with sentiment. They were in deadly earnest. Their subjects were the Wounded Warrior[1] (*21*), half reclining in an unnatural attitude meant to express anguish, an emotion unknown in Greek art of the High Classical period, or the

[1] In the Archaeological Museum, Venice.

Fighting Gaul,[1] that fine fragment from waist to knees, clad in tight trousers, striding forward, the muscles rippling, thighs firm and loins taut in a final vehement effort for survival.

By the beginning of the second century A.D. the Pergamese builders were in the throes of an ambitious town planning in which their Baroque sculpture formed a prominent part of the composition. As distinct from earlier Greek cities whose principal buildings were crammed together with no apparent regard for siting—the Athens Acropolis instances this (*24*)—the buildings of Pergamum were grouped in careful relation to the steep physical setting and united one to another with graceful steps. Although town planning is one of the concomitants of Baroque architecture in the Italian seventeenth century, there are no traces of Baroque design in the remnants of Pergamese houses. Nor does it appear that the great base for the altar of Zeus Soter (*c.* 188 B.C.) which the early Christians were to regard as the Throne of the Devil, with its gigantic sculptural adornment of the Battle of the Gods with the Giants, a terrifying agglomeration of winged and draperied figures and writhing snakes in a deep unbroken band, was anything but classical and staid.

In plan and elevation Greek buildings never digressed from the norm of the earliest temples, established half a millennium before the fifth century B.C. With the Parthenon the slow perfection of the Doric order had reached its apogee. Frank Granger[2] saw in its creator (whom he took to be the sculptor-architect Phidias[3]) the forerunner of Michelangelo and Bernini in that he was moved by pictorial considerations. If the introduction of a third dimension could mean that an artist was Baroque, then indeed the architect of the Parthenon might be so named. For if ever a building were plastic, in the round, it is the Parthenon. The architect has deliberately set out to deceive the eye by sheer enchantment—or to be more specific, by a mastery of the scientific laws of optics. His knowledge

[1] In the Metropolitan Museum, New York.

[2] Frank Granger, The Parthenon and the Baroque: *Journal of the Royal Institute of British Architects*, 17 October 1931.

[3] According to Plutarch Callicrates and Ictinus were the joint architects; but Phidias was Pericles's superintendent of all public buildings in Athens.

of projection has enabled him to convey by a forward slant of the high entablature a sense of the strictest verticality. He has, contrariwisely, made all the columns incline a slight degree towards the interior, those at the four corners doubly so. Also by thickening the four corner columns which, the eye declares, carry most of the burden, he has succeeded not in accentuating their apparent diameter as might be thought but in giving them the semblance of an equal size to the others. Furthermore by laying the horizontal steps along slightly convex lines, calculated to an extreme nicety, he has made the heavy weight of the seemingly regular structure come to life, with the result that the longer one looks at it the more it palpitates. Plutarch may have been aware of these ingenious devices when he referred to the Parthenon in the following words: "An indefinite novelty keeps the building untouched by time as though the work had a spirit which always flowered and a soul which never grew old." By less subtle magic perhaps but with no less technical mastery of the science of construction the Italian Baroque age first revived the architecture of the Ancients and then developed it far beyond what they had contemplated or would have approved.

If I am over-refining the term Baroque by applying it to the Parthenon—or indeed any Greek Doric temple of the High Classical age—I have rather more justification for associating it with its neighbour, the Erectheum. This temple is said to have been begun twenty-six years later than the other and finished about 407 B.C., which makes it a contemporary of the Niobe group and the Victory of the Stoa of Zeus. A first sight of the Erectheum may even lead one to suppose that its designer had lost that sense of form innate in practically every Greek artist. To begin with, his plan although strictly composed of straight lines, is highly eccentric. This is not entirely due to the steep slope and the two floor levels on which the Erectheum is constructed. Features have been wilfully imposed upon the architecture not for utility but for effect. The west façade consists of an engaged portico which can serve no practical purpose whatever and is solely aesthetic. The famous Porch of the Maidens seems quite unrelated to the south front and

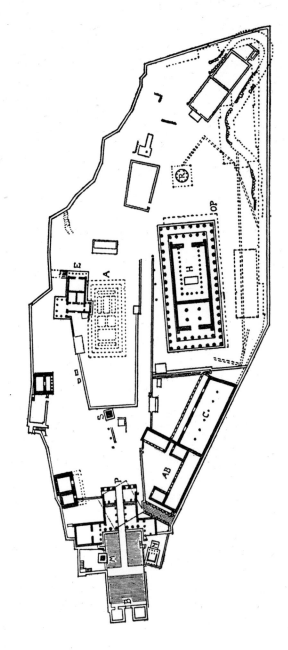

24   *Plan of the Acropolis at Athens, Restored*

its asymmetrical siting can at best be termed pictorial. The caryatids, or maidens, which struck some contemporaries as most unjustifiable innovations, give the impression of sculpture carved from the living rock. Moreover the temple was the most profusely ornate of any up to then. The chromatic materials, a black Eleusian limestone as a background to white marble relief on the friezes, and the jewel-like carving of naturalistic ornament seem more Corinthian than Ionic, and were a complete departure from any previous architectural practice.

If Greek buildings never attained that development of style which we recognize as full Baroque, those of the Romans certainly did so. Whereas, curiously enough, Hellenistic sculpture was Baroque, late Roman sculpture was not. On the contrary it was derivative and uninspired and for the most part coarsely executed. Its sole excellence was in the portrait bust. The Romans may never have infused into their architecture the almost magical or spiritual quality of the Parthenon—the result of a slow perfecting over the centuries of a single disciplined formula—but they evolved styles more freely and rapidly than the Greeks. The Corinthian order which they originated lent itself to higher decorative treatment than the Doric and Ionic. The Romans were besides great technicians and engineers. They invented the rounded arch, the theatrical scene and the dome, perhaps the most pictorial—certainly the most poetical—achievement of western architecture and they experimented widely in planning and town development. All these inventions led to a kind of Baroque expression.

As in the case of Greek art, the further from the fatherland the freer did this expression tend to become. Generally speaking, most Baroque Roman buildings to survive are found in the outposts of the Roman Empire. Compared with the sedate Augustan triumphal arches of the Roman Forum and even with the fourth-century Arch of Constantine, the Arch of Tiberius at Orange seems full of animation, with its prominent entablature and, on each side face, a quite unclassical lunette thrust into the tympanum of the pediment (*23*). The spaces over the heads are filled with carved military trophies deeply undercut. The whole structure is free and joyous as though the old Romans knew that, as well as raising a commemorative arch, they were marking the entry to the spendid south at this most romantically named spot where the frigid north is finally left behind, the olive is first seen, the cicada first heard and where since time immemorial the staple produce has been millet stalks for brooms, wool, silk, honey and truffles. At Aspendus in Pamphylia, the second-century theatre back scene, with its two orders of projecting columns in pairs and central broken pediment, flanked by pointed and semi-circular lesser pediments, commanded a magnificent and highly decorative theme. Only the dome seems not to have excelled in the colonies. In Rome itself Hadrian's Pantheon dome, a miracle of engineering, remains intact to this day, having been an object of wonder and admiration to all Renaissance church builders from Brunelleschi onwards. Dome designs were of course to be greatly improved and developed in daring by the Baroque architects.

At Baalbec in the Middle East the early second-century Temple of Venus, with its round-headed niches and encircling columns supporting an entablature in deep concave loops, is about the most

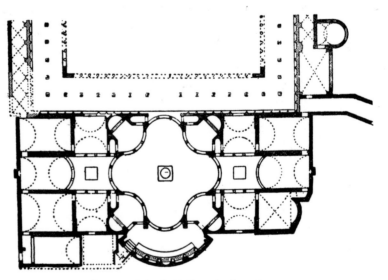

25   *Hadrian's Villa: the Vestibule*

strikingly Baroque of all Roman buildings (*22*). Hardly less so, although two hundred years later, is the Mausoleum at Spalato in Dalmatia within the vast Palace of Diocletian. The interior of this temple has two stages of projecting columns, Corinthian below, Ionic above, with wall niches in between, and was clearly designed to benefit from the changing play of light and shade. As an example of Roman colonial town planning we have at Silchester in remote Britain a checkboard pattern of streets and squares within a pentagonal walled enclosure. All of these diverse features we shall come upon throughout the seventeenth and eighteenth centuries as symbolic of Baroque architecture.

If the majority of the colonial buildings just referred to can never have been seen by seventeenth-century Romans (whose travels were far more circumscribed than those of their ancient forebears) there were several vestiges of late Imperial architecture in and around Rome itself. Of them Hadrian's Villa at Tivoli was one of the most accessible. The planning of its several rooms is also highly eccentric. For example, the two vestibules off the Piazza d'Oro are shaped, the one in a sinuous outline of convexities and concavities (*25*), the other with alternate rectangular and semi-circular recesses. It is not surprising that the seventeenth century interested itself in the more bizarre of such structures. Sir Anthony Blunt[1] has lately drawn attention to the wide circulation of the extraordinary drawings and designs of G. B. Montani, a Milanese carver and sculptor in wood and stone. When Montani died in 1621 at an advanced age he left his papers to his pupil Soria, who assembled them for publication in 1684 under the familiar and unpromising title *I Cinque Libri di Architettura*. Doubtless the originals were handled by architects long before that date. In the second book, entitled *Scielta de Varii Tempietti Antichi*, Montani gives numerous eccentric plans of temples—many on the Via Appia—which he claims to have seen excavated and which he recorded before their destruction. In addition he reproduces what he conjectures were their elevations. These often assume such truly amazing outlines that one is impelled

[1] In a lecture at the Courtauld Institute, 1956.

seriously to question their probability. Many of them are what we would certainly style Baroque.[1] But since Montani's plans of surviving ancient buildings are accurate we have no reason to assume that those of buildings which have disappeared are necessarily inaccurate. In any case some of his plans—notably those of two temples in the neighbourhood of Tivoli—are reflected in the buildings of Bernini and Borromini such as the strange curved wall behind the church at Ariccia and the cupola of S. Andrea delle Fratte.[2]

Cardinals and Princes of seventeenth-century Rome collected antique sculpture in great abundance. Scipione Borghese (*42*), Cardinal-Secretary to Pope Paul V in the first quarter of the century, assembled an unrivalled collection in the Casino Borghese, much of which remains there today. The Ludovisi, Barberini and Pamphili papal nephews followed suit on a hardly less splendid scale. So did some of the most successful sculptors and architects like Della Porta, Bernini and Ferrata, as we know from an inventory of the possessions of the last taken after his death. Those collectors who were neither rich nor influential enough to acquire original fragments would hasten to have copies made or casts taken of important pieces as they were excavated. Sometimes they commissioned sculptors to produce for them modern versions of the gods of mythology. In this way Cardinal Scipione bought from Bernini some of his most famous groups, still in the Casino Borghese. As well as modelling from the antique, artists of repute did not consider it beneath them to restore missing heads and arms to ancient torsos, as Algardi did to Hercules killing the Hydra. Nor did they scruple deliberately to copy from these sources. Algardi reproduced the Hercules and Hydra in relief upon the collar of Urbano Millini's bust in S. Maria del Popolo, and Bernini took the head of the Apollo Belvedere for that of his Apollo chasing Daphne (*26, 27*). The very poses of antique

[1] The 4th Book, entitled *Diversi Ornamenti Capricciosi*, contains Montani's own designs for altars and reredoses which, curiously enough, are not the least Baroque but Mannerist and typical of the age he lived in.

[2] Several of Montani's original drawings, now in the Soane Museum, were bought by Sir John Soane at the Adam Sale, and it is not far-fetched to see in one of them the possible derivation of Robert Adam's hall at Kedleston.

figures were adapted to modern subjects. Cordier's bust of St. Paul (in S. Paolo fuori le mura) is taken from that of an ancient philosopher, and Bernini's Sebastian seems to reflect the attitude of the Barberini Faun. Bernini and Algardi, commissioned to produce a memorial statue of Urban VIII's brother, Carlo Barberini, even went so far as to acquire an antique torso of Julius Caesar and add to it a head and legs in the likeness of the deceased.

Every Baroque sculptor and architect began his career by studying and drawing from the antique. For this purpose all the private collections of Rome were available to young artists. Access was seldom, if ever, refused. For three years of his youth Bernini walked each morning from his father's house near S. Maria Maggiore to the Vatican, where he drew antique statues till sundown, deriving, he tells us, his only source of warmth in the cold winter months from a few husks of bread and a cup of wine. As a result of a general immersion in the antique, artists tended to represent the Christian saints in the guise of the ancient gods. So seriously did the Jesuits regard this misleading form of hagiography that the famous Father General, Oliva, felt obliged to thunder denunciations from the pulpit. The popular conception of the Apostles and Fathers of the Church was, he cried, being corrupted by these heathen images and thereby the meaning of the Holy Gospels stood in danger of gross abuse and misrepresentation.

RELIGION, THE CHURCH AND THE JESUITS

With a true understanding of the Antique, which men of the Baroque shared with men of the Renaissance, there went a contrasting devotion to the Faith which was only shared in intensity with men of mediaeval times. It was of course very largely induced by the shock of the Reformation and was in a sense a substitute for the Humanism of the Renaissance. Padre Oliva need not have worked himself into a state of alarm for, had he only known it, the seeming new paganism was really the old gothic fervour speaking through a classical idiom; it was the invasion of classical forms by the mediaeval spirit. The

Baroque was in other words the issue of the Christian Faith re-
generated, and not of heathen mythology. This regeneration of the
Faith was in its turn conceived of a Spanish form of mysticism
brought to the peninsula by the Emperor Charles V and fostered
by the followers of Ignatius Loyola. It was, then, the consequence of
the Church's struggle for survival in the sixteenth century, and not
the process of that struggle which had coincided with Mannerism.
The Baroque expressed "the heroism of sacrifice as contrasted with
the classical heroism of earthly life and human ambition and fulfilment"[1] which had distinguished both pagan and Renaissance
ideologies.

Bramante's Renaissance and Palladio's Vitruvianism may be
termed cultural revivals—the one an immediate, the other a belated,
consequence of the Humanism which the scholars of the thirteenth
and fourteenth centuries had sprung upon the world by rediscovering
the learning of the ancients. They were therefore essentially pagan.
The Baroque was more than these in that it was a religious inspiration. Its architects piled order upon order to achieve the old mediaeval
verticality which had been the mightiest expression of the Christian
endeavour towards union with God. Their technical prowess was as
great as their power of invention. It took a new form, that of drawing
the eye up to the height of vault and dome which were appropriately
decorated. This was a principle much emphasized by the Jesuits who
realized that faith was stifled inside a bare basilica. So they frequently
had painted a feigned open sky against which were depicted scenes
of ecstatic mysticism made memorable by the early saints of their
Society.

The devotion of the Baroque artists to their faith was genuine
and concerted. We know how Michelangelo had become obsessed
with the salvation of his soul. Carlo Dolci would only paint subjects
that might provoke religious contemplation. Luca Giordano would
not travel to Spain without his confessor. Tiepolo belonged to the
Confraternity of Mount Carmel. Jean Boucher was extremely
devout; he kept his studio in one of the towers of Bourges Cathedral

[1] E. I. Watkin, "British Baroque", *Church Quarterly Review*, April 1946.

26 *Head of Apollo, from Bernini's Apollo and Daphne. (Villa Borghese, Rome)*

27 *Head of the Apollo Belvedere (Vatican Galleries)*

28 *A Design, by Ferdinando Bibiena, for a new theatre in Bologna,*
to be opened in 1703

and would only work for churches and convents.[1] None of the Baroque religious painters, it is true, chose the subjects he had to depict for a sacred edifice. These were always dictated by the patron who commissioned them, as we may readily conclude from the esoteric ecclesiastical character they usually assumed. We cannot imagine the simple artist working out undirected the particular mystic symbolism of some obscure patron saint which a minor religious order wanted represented on ceiling or reredos. In this sense the Church may have made art into an instrument of propaganda. It is more correct to say that it helped to fashion art in its own likeness and so enriched God's temples in deliberate answer to the Protestant challenge. Artists were required to proclaim through their skill the dogmas of the Catholic Faith, and eagerly agreed to do it. That an institution so firmly based on tradition could mould such astonishingly unconventional artists as Caravaggio, Bernini and Borromini, is alone a sufficient rebuttal of the frequent charge that the Catholic Church deprived the seventeenth century of frank utterance and freedom of creation. It is absolutely impossible to wrest works of genius from unwilling mediums.

Emile Mâle in his exhaustive study of the numerous religious subjects depicted in the seventeenth century has shown how the Counter-reformation Church laid most emphasis on two dogmas, both of which strike at the very roots of Protestantism. They are Charity and the Blessed Sacrament. Charles Borromeo, the most popular Italian saint of the sixteenth century, embodied to a remarkable degree the virtues which the Counter-reformation extolled. He was the greatest of the fighters against Protestantism, for he advocated all those dogmas which the Protestants attacked, namely the cult of our Lady, the primacy of St. Peter, the efficacy of prayers for the dead, the intervention of the saints, veneration of images and relics, martyrdom as the crowning glory—and, in particular, Charity and the Blessed Sacrament. These mysteries, and above all the two last, were represented in Baroque churches. The emphasis on Charity, or good works, was specially directed against the Lutheran heresy of

[1] Emile Mâle, *L'Art Religieux du XVIIe Siècle*, 1932.

Justification by Faith alone. This dismal precept which taught that, since man was in very essence evil, no charitable actions could be considered disinterested in God's eyes and therefore his only hope of salvation lay in an implicit obedience, was strongly opposed by the Saint and the Counter-reformation clergy. They taught that, on the contrary, faith by itself was not enough and that man could only be saved by the additional practice of acts of mercy and charity. Hence the numerous paintings and reliefs portraying St. Charles bringing comfort and hope to the plague stricken, St. Martin sharing his cloak with the beggar and St. Elizabeth of Portugal tending the sick.

The solemnization of the Blessed Sacrament was even more in evidence since it was the very lynch pin of the revived Catholic faith. Though the Last Supper had in previous centuries been frequently depicted, the moment chosen was usually that of Judas's betrayal. Now it was the moment of the consecration of the Host, held aloft for all to behold—a scene, curiously enough, less often represented in the Middle Ages, presumably because it was considered too sacred.

Whereas the Middle Ages had concentrated upon straightforward miracles, the raising of Lazarus from the dead or the turning of the water into wine at Cana, the Counter-reformation now sought to win a rather more sophisticated congregation to whom these evidences of the supreme power were no longer sufficiently alluring or convincing. Instead it dwelt upon incidents of ecstasy and mysticism in the lives of holy men and women in order by these means to impress the bulk of the people who, it must be remembered, still could neither read nor understand except through pictures and images. To this extent the Baroque was a didactic art.

Earlier historians of seventeenth-century art clearly misread its meaning when they wrote that "the defect of Baroque lies in its blatant materialism".[1] Pronouncements such as this were a legacy from the intense antipathy towards the Baroque of the late eighteenth century, nauseated after two hundred years by the style's over-

[1] M. S. Briggs, *Baroque Architecture*, 1913.

abundance and final decline into cheap pomposity. Milizia,[1] writing in 1797 when the Neo-classical revival was in full swing, called excess of ornamentation for its own sake the chief abuse of the Baroque. He condemned the seventeenth century as *secola della bizzaria*. In his view it was bent upon gratifying the senses rather than fulfilling the final purposes of art, which presumably he considered to be the edification of the mind. This spark of Puritanism was fanned to fury in the nineteenth century. Arthur Hugh Clough expressed Victorian sentiments on the Baroque in a scream of moral indignation which in a muddled way is directed against the Jesuits as the cause of it:

"Here with emasculate pupils and gimcrack churches of Gesù,
Pseudo-learning and lies, confessional-boxes and postures,—
Here, with metallic beliefs and regimental devotions,—
Here, overcrusting with slime, perverting, defacing, debasing . . ."

No words seemed strong enough for his condemnation of the Holy City. He continued:

"Rome disappoints me much; I hardly as yet understand, but *Rubbishy* seems the word that most exactly would suit it."

The nineteenth-century antipathy was based on a disbelief that the religious fervour of the Baroque generations could be sincere. Somerset Maugham[2] is still uneasy. He finds "their religion declamatory", which he explains by reason of their being unsure of their belief: they sought to drown their hesitations by feigning what they did not really feel, but what the Counter-reformation Church obliged them to express. This cautious disapproval is understandable and comes from the inability of the reticent Protestant to sympathize with the articulate Catholic, especially when practical considerations are brought into play.

After all, the Anglican Bishop Burnet travelling in Italy during James II's reign exhibited exactly the same uneasiness. In Milan he

---

[1] Fráncesco Milizia, *Memorie degli Architetti Antichi e Moderni*, 1797.
[2] W. Somerset Maugham, *Don Fernando*, 1935.

witnessed a scene that genuinely shocked him. A Capuchin preacher mounted the pulpit and in a torrent of emotion and rhetoric seized a crucifix which he hugged and kissed in transports, but not without first having blown the dust off it. Such behaviour, the Bishop argued, must be disingenuous. He was also much scandalized by "statues with nudities" in the Medici Chapel and the prodigious display of silver plate, more fit for the house of a prince than of God.

Rudolph Wittkower[1] has issued a warning against regarding all religious art of the seventeenth century as borrowed from the theatre. That the Jesuits introduced stage mechanism and devices into their churches is quite another matter which I shall touch upon directly. Meanwhile we cannot overlook the deep religious mysticism of the Baroque age which was expressed by extremely fervent attitudes. Bernini's St. Teresa in S. Maria della Vittoria is no more dramatized than were the actual mystical experiences of the Saint of Avila, which were the sequel to spiritual exercises of the most exacting kind that the soul and indeed the human body can submit to.

The extreme spiritual ardour of the time led to a belief that the supernatural was the normal. The visionary, ecstatic life was so deeply impressed upon the beholder every time he entered a church that he came to see in it the obvious explanation of the universal order of things. Consequently a sort of pantheism developed out of the Baroque. Art no longer interpreted nature; the rôles were reversed and nature was seen in terms of art. Whereas the Renaissance believed that the column was derived from the tree trunk, the Baroque made their columns turn into trees, like Daphne into a laurel bush. The Italian Jesuit Bartoli, while watching a sunset, was not induced to meditate upon the eternal marvels of God's handiwork in contrast with the transitoriness of man's efforts, nor of course to enjoy the aerial beauty displayed before his eyes. Instead, the sunset recalled to him the gilded glories and stucco angels which were being fashioned in the Roman churches around him. In a similar paradoxical sense death came to be more real than life itself. It was an obsession, and not a happy one, because man never arrived

[1] R. Wittkower, *Bernini, The Sculptor of the Roman Baroque*, 1955.

at a reconciliation with its horrors. The Renaissance had given a serenity and peace to death, a state not at all to be dreaded. Its monuments depicted the deceased as a hero recumbent in sleep or reclining like some ancient Greek or Roman at a banquet. Its paintings of martyrs showed them in complacent attitudes with perhaps at the side some attribute of their end discreetly introduced. With the turn of the seventeenth century, however, the character of monuments changes, or rather reverts to that of the Middle Ages. Death is no longer static but full of terror and movement. In place of the emaciated Gothic cadaver supine beneath the figure of Abbot or Crusader, grinning skulls and menacing skeletons now emerge from half-open tombs. Bernini in his monument to Urban VIII (*31*) in St. Peter's included the triumphant skeleton, and in his Raimondi memorial in S. Pietro in Montorio a relief of corpses being eaten by worms. Nor were men in the full bloom of life allowed to forget the fate awaiting them. Innocent IX kept before him a conjectural portrait of himself on his deathbed; Alexander VII, the descendant of the sybaritic patron of Raphael, kept his coffin under the bed and drank out of a skull; Padre Oliva peered every day into a tomb with a decomposing corpse inside it, and Father Cajetan preferred to sleep with his head on a skull rather than a pillow. Architecture too found a use in human skulls and bones in place of stone and stucco with which to build and decorate the walls of chapels, as we may see in the Cappella di S. Bernardino alle Ossa in Milan.

Never did a period concentrate more upon the very action of dying. It derived from the moment of the soul's departure from the body a savage grandeur, of which there is strong enough evidence in Shakespeare's plays. Painters went to great lengths to study how men met a barbarous end in order to give their martyrdoms every realistic appearance. They frequented public executions and dissected corpses. Callot's drawings of hanged men bear witness to his close study of the subject. Germain Pilon's sculptured corpses are brutally realistic, and Caravaggio's and Ribera's scenes of death are no less representational. With this morbid concentration upon death went that indifference towards human, and certainly animal suffering, which constitutes one of the least appealing attributes of Roman Catholicism to this day. The Baroque was not a tender movement. It had no use for the homely and in its Nativity scenes, for example, the patient donkey and other farmyard animals were now omitted as being beneath the dignity of Our Lord's companionship.[1] The mean of everyday life and gentle conduct was eschewed. The Baroque pendulum was one of extremes which swung backwards and forwards between ruthlessness and splendour.

No doubt the Jesuits were largely responsible for the emphasis of these extremes. Ignatius Loyola's *Spiritual Exercises* had a tremendous hold upon the intelligentsia. In its concentration upon ultimate physical mortality the book sought to discipline men's minds by a constant reminder of what awaited unbelievers—namely an eternity of posthumous reprisals—and the faithful at the opposite celestial pole—the glorious rewards depicted upon church domes and vaults. The *Spiritual Exercises* was certainly the origin of the hauntingly realistic manifestations of death. In Bernini, the greatest sculptor of the Baroque age, it had an apt disciple. He was the artist most responsible for death scenes in marble. All his life he was a devoted friend of the Jesuits and a pious follower of the *Spiritual Exercises*, a cult he shared with two other great pioneers of the Baroque movement, namely El Greco and Rubens. In fact one of the chief reasons why Bernini came to the fore as a very young man was that his Jesuit training earned him the sympathy of Gregory XV who canonized St. Ignatius.

As early as 1620 the anonymous author of a *Discourse of Rome* published in London[2] spoke of the Jesuit churches as being of special renown for their splendour. He told of "all possible inventions to catch men's affections and to ravish their understanding", notably their glorious altars, the infinite number of their images, their priestly vestments, not to mention their "divers actions" in celebrat-

[1] The touching scene of the fifteenth-century Colantonio's picture of St. Jerome (Capodimonte Museum, Naples) wherein the Saint is extracting a thorn from one of the paws of the docile lion—the other paw resting on the Saint's lap—could never have been recorded in Baroque times.

[2] From "Collected Essays" in *Horae Subsecivae*, Anon 1620.

ing Mass, the miracles they counterfeited and the exquisite music
they provided. One of their inventions was of course the adoption
of theatrical machinery and the various paraphernalia of the
stage. They enlisted the services of the famous Bibiena family.
Ferdinando Bibiena made stage-sets for two Jesuit seminaries in
Bologna where they had theatres for training preachers in dramatic
delivery (*28*). In S. Francesco a Ripa in Rome, there exists a cunning
mechanism for shifting wings and back drop and opening up panels
and pilasters which disclose eighteen thousand relics. The *teatra sacra*,
or religious peepshow, and the *castra doloris*, a huge catafalque
for the royal dead crested with flaming urns and a figure of
Father Time with his scythe, of which the Bibienas were past
masters in construction, were largely of Jesuit contrivance and
became especially popular with the Viennese court in the eighteenth
century. One of the grandest spectacles of the age was Pozzo's
ephemeral theatre representing the Marriage at Cana set up in the
Gesù in 1685. A range of perspective arches fitted with thousands of
concealed candles illuminated clouds on which sat angels adoring the
Blessed Sacrament.

I have already referred to the brave ornamentation of the Gesù—
mostly imposed after the *Horae Subsecivae* was published. Ocular
tricks and decorative legerdemain of all sorts are what the Society
delighted in. It seldom failed to make the most of them because it
well knew how best to capture the wonder and attention of the
masses. In the Gesuiti in Venice (*29*) the walls, seemingly hung with a
white and green figured damask, are really of marble; the tawny
turkey carpet with its creases and folds in front of the altar is
likewise a piece of make-believe in the same material. But the fact
that the Jesuits with their subtle understanding of human nature
fully exploited several aspects of Baroque art does not mean that they
were in any sense the source of it. Pastor in his *History of the Popes*[1]
strongly denies it. He points out that they readily adopted whatever
style was current. They built, for example, churches in Cologne and

---

[1] Ludwig F. von Pastor, *History of the Popes*, vols. 25–31 (1605–76), ed.
1939.

Molsheim in an antiquated mediaeval style with the merest traces of German Renaissance detail introduced, long after the Gothic had been abandoned in the Latin countries of Europe.

POPES AND PATRONS

Neither is it correct to state that the Papacy was the sole source of the Baroque. On the other hand it was the mainspring of the movement in that individual Popes happened to play a close personal part in the patronage and development of seventeenth-century Roman art. A succession of remarkably cultivated men in the Chair of St. Peter was the artists' greatest good fortune. Without the sun of papal encouragement the genius of Bernini and Borromini would not have had the same chances to ripen. A further factor of significance is that the vicissitudes of the Roman Baroque coincided with the rise, climax and decline of the Papacy as a temporal power during the difficult readjustment of European politics after the Counter-reformation. For this reason the Baroque may perhaps be termed the art of great rulers. Clement X (Altieri) who reigned from 1670 to 1676 was the last seventeenth-century pontiff to patronize architecture and soon after his death the prestige of the Papacy began sharply to decline. The Jesuits were by now widely disliked and distrusted and the powerful secular princes were hamstringing the authority of the Church.

During the first three-quarters of the seventeenth century the occupants of the papal throne were as astute as they were artistic. But what chiefly distinguished them was their unassumed piety and their ceaseless struggle to maintain peace in Christendom. Clement IX was practically a saint, and Clement X a man of angelic character, even though they were not as intellectual as their immediate predecessors. One and all exhausted themselves in an endeavour to keep the Catholic powers united in resistance to Protestant aggression. It is noteworthy that while Europe was in the grip of the Thirty Years War the Papal States remained free from combat apart from a single domestic incident involving a short, sharp contest with Duke Odoardo Farnese over the fief of Castro, in which there was one

29   *Gesuiti, Venice: the Pulpit. The "damask" hangings*
are of marble

30 *The figure of Fortezza, one of the fountains at the Quadrivio delle Quattro Fontane, Rome*
Carlo Fontana, architect

31 *Tomb (1639–47) of Pope Urban VIII in St. Peter's, Rome*
G. L. Bernini, sculptor

casualty! But the unremitting dissension between the two leading powers, France and Spain, in which both treated the Papacy as a catspaw, dismissed the last hopes of a united Christendom at the very moment when the course of the War was going favourably. The flaunting of the juridical rights of the Church by Venice (tantamount to a schism) covertly fostered by the English Ambassador, Wotton, during the pontificate of Paul V, was as nothing compared with Spain's interference with papal policy and the diabolical machinations first of Richelieu, then of Mazarin, during the reign of Urban VIII and his successors. France, with the unashamed cynicism we associate with Gallicanism, in the course of creating for herself an absolute state and of dismembering the Holy Roman Empire to boot, cajoled, bullied and deceived the Papacy to an extent which was only paralleled by Hitler's methods with Czechoslovakia and Poland in our own time. No wonder that with the subordination of ideals to power politics by the two leading Catholic nations the cause of the Church against the Protestant heresy was permanently weakened through the Treaty of Westphalia.

The five pontiffs who reigned longest during the Baroque supremacy happened to be the most learned and cultivated. Paul V (1605–21) numbered among his personal friends eminent scholars such as Baronius the historian, Federigo Borromeo, founder of the Ambrosian Library, Bellarmine, the Jesuit controversialist, and Galileo, whom he received with honour. His favourable encouragement of the arts and architecture was however prompted less by personal taste than political motive. During his long pontificate the decision was taken to demolish the remains of Constantine's basilica of St. Peter's owing to its unsafe condition and to impose Maderna's substitute and façade. Three thousand labourers were engaged and the Pope was present on every critical occasion. During operations Paul showed far greater respect for the monuments of the past than his Renaissance predecessors. He decreed that every care must be taken of the shrines of the saints and he had drawings and records made of all that was destroyed. He repaired aqueducts, planned new streets, and built fountains and churches. His Cappella Paolina in S. Maria

Maggiore is reckoned the most sumptuous and over-loaded architecture of his reign (*33*). It is typical of the man, although less typical of the age, for it is not yet fully Baroque. Compared with the Cappella Sistina of a previous generation which it balances, it is brilliant and alive, but its particular excellencies (notably the reliefs) are lost in a polychrome rash of marbles like jewels sewn into the superabundant folds of embroidered hangings.

Maffeo Barberini, Urban VIII (1623–44), the patron and intimate of Bernini, who in later life never tired of quoting his master's sallies and repartee, was of course one of the greatest followers Maecenas ever had. There will be frequent references to his activities throughout these pages. This formidable prince of the Church, with his olive complexion, black square beard, thick hair streaked with silver, lofty forehead, bushy eyebrows and shrewd blue eyes is probably better known to us than any European figure of the seventeenth century owing to his numerous portraits, not to mention busts (*31*). His wit, acumen and self-reliance have not endeared him to Protestant historians and his blameless life has done nothing to dispel his unpopularity. Immensely erudite, he was a poet of considerable distinction and during the worst crises of his reign would still compose and have read to him the verse of his contemporaries, whom he encouraged to write about Christianity rather than Classical mythology. His Latin compositions were perhaps his best and were translated into many languages and set to music. Music was the other art most dear to him. Gregorio Allegri, priest and tenor singer, whom he made a member of the papal choir, composed the famous *Miserere* for double choir, which, in spite of a decree that the score should never be reproduced, Mozart, so it is said, a hundred and forty years later wrote down after a single hearing in the Sistine Chapel. Urban made Girolamo Frescobaldi, the renowned virtuoso, organist of St. Peter's and thirty thousand people flocked to the basilica the first time he performed there. Paolo Agostino, to whom the Pope after a special Mass once turned and bowed, was his choirmaster. When a new breviary was compiled Urban personally corrected and rearranged the hymns in a Baroque dress.

Although a new Baroque music had evolved earlier in the century with Giovanni Gabrieli, one of the founders of choral and orchestral composition, the colour of whose vocal and instrumental ensembles recalls the warm rich tones of his compatriot, Titian, and with Claudio Monteverdi, who revived the spirit of antique tragedy by the creation of musical dissonance and drama, Baroque ritual first appeared in Rome in Urban's reign. It was characterized by the use of new instruments of four strings, by polyphony and by oratorios. These were at first performed in churches with action, scenery and stage costume, a musical elaboration as it were of the mediaeval mystery plays. The oratorio which is usually looked upon as a northern manifestation actually originated in the church of St. Philip Neri at the beginning of the century as a method of dramatic vocal statement of religious belief, in contrast to the coeval opera, which was secular. In the following century it became extremely popular in Germany through the Passion Music of Bach and reached its most triumphant expression in Great Britain with Handel.

Urban was the patron of all learning. He encouraged the Jesuit Bollandus's great undertaking, the *Acta Sanctorum*, or collection of biographies and legends of the Saints.[1] He made Holstentius, a scholar of international renown, keeper of the Barberini Library. Ever since his cardinalate he had been a wholehearted admirer of Galileo and encouraged him to write the book[2] which so gravely offended the Inquisition. To Urban's deep personal distress he felt obliged to let the great astronomer be summoned before that reactionary body; he even suffered him to be convicted of heresy for accepting the prohibited Copernican system that the planets revolved round the sun and not the earth. In this matter Urban committed an egregious folly and made himself ridiculous in the eyes of posterity. His weakness was all the more distressing because several enlightened Cardinals secretly approved Galileo's ideas. Moreover Galileo, who was no disbeliever, professed to be seeking the

---

[1] It is still in progress at Louvain and must surely be the longest unbroken work of scholarship in Europe.

[2] *Dialogo dei due Massimi sistemi del Mondo*, published in Florence, 1632.

divine explanation of things through the study of scientific laws, just as Caravaggio did later through a realistic interpretation of nature in painting.

Innocent X, Pamphili (1644–55) (*32*), with his lean, grave, suspicious face immortalized by Velasquez—*Troppo vero,* as he said of his portrait—had none of the panache of his predecessor. Although he had little liking for literature he encouraged scholarly research in the Vatican archives. He showed great interest in the improvements to St. Peter's and commissioned Borromini to transform the interior of St. John Lateran. To him are thus due the opportunities granted to the most creative architect of the Baroque age. The architect Rainaldi and sculptor Algardi were likewise patronized by Innocent, and the Villa and the Palazzo Pamphili are the enduring monuments of his reign.

Alexander VII, Chigi (1655–67), left an indelible mark on the City as we see from the Chigi crest of six hills surmounted by a star which crowns a number of churches, obelisks and gateways. He completed the Sapienza, or Roman University, and founded the Libreria Alessandrina. He had the Chigi Chapel in S. Maria del Popolo restored by Bernini and then the whole church with the help of the Lombard sculptor, Antonio Raggi. He employed Bernini again to add the façade and gallery to his country residence at Castel Gandolfo and to build the church in the little town. He was responsible for Bernini's great colonnade in the piazza of St. Peter's as well as other stupendous works by the master. They include the Cathedra in the extreme west end of the basilica, to which Alexander presented the red damask hangings with gold fringes used to this day to drape the pilasters on special festivals. His admiration for and friendship with Bernini were as cordial as Urban's and he frequently paid visits to the architect's studio.

All the important institutions in Rome benefited under this enlightened pontiff whose zeal for reform was as sincere as his concern for the welfare of his temporal subjects. He was a man of unaffected piety and, more important still, of wide human understanding and gentleness. His finely cut features, high forehead and delicate physique proclaimed the intellectual. Like Pope Urban he was no inconsiderable poet and so devoted was he to the Muses that even in the height of summer he would forego his siesta in order to read and discuss verse with his friends. Only by this means was he able to forget the endless anxieties caused him by the intrigues of Louis XIV and the Jansenist heresy, and to be happy. His reign marked the golden age of learning and the arts, its meridian and also its swansong. For with the saintly Clement IX, Rospigliosi—who reigned but two years from 1667–69—and Clement X, Altieri (1670–76) the end of the Roman High Baroque was in sight. Clement X was the last of the seventeenth-century Popes to regard the arts as a paramount means of enhancing the prestige of the Papacy and so of enlisting the devotion of Catholics to the Faith. He ordered Carlo Rainaldi to add the tribune end of S. Maria Maggiore and had Bernini's precious tabernacle erected in the Chapel of the Blessed Sacrament of St. Peter's. The election through French intrigue of Cardinal Albani in 1700 as Clement XI marked the end of the High Baroque in Rome.

What individual Popes from lack of sufficient leisure were unable to achieve in way of art patronage was made good by their Cardinal nephews. For in an age when patronage counted for everything, as soon as a new representative ascended the throne of St. Peter a host of satellite relations revolved round him, coruscating in his glory which they knew only too well might be of limited duration owing to the usually advanced age of a Pope upon his election. At his death they were at once eclipsed by the family of his successor, and then made off with as much booty as they had had the astuteness to amass in the fleeting interlude. The consequence was that a succession of Cardinals Borghese, Ludovisi, Barberini, Pamphili, Chigi, Rospigliosi and Altieri, enriched by indulgent uncles, became lavish patrons of artists, built themselves palaces which today are the glory of Rome and filled them with collections of pictures, statuary and works of art of every description. Often a single Pope had as many as three or even four Cardinal nephews who vied with each other for his favour and their enrichment. Frequently these nephews arrogated to themselves authority which the Popes deeply resented; but so engrained was the custom of nepotism that no amount of displeasure or threats put the slightest check upon their activities and greed. For the most part the Cardinal nephews were feared and flattered in their zenith and reviled and even persecuted after their fall. Only the Rospigliosi and Altieri families, because of their comparative modesty and tact, earned themselves a measure of respect and tolerance.

Outside the families of the reigning Popes the most prodigal patron of the arts in seventeenth-century Rome was undoubtedly Queen Christina of Sweden, the last of the Vasas. This extraordinary woman, who abdicated the throne in July, 1654, and travelled in male attire to Innsbruck where she solemnly made her profession of the Catholic Faith, reached Rome in the following December. There she drove by night from the Porta del Popolo between rows of torches to the Vatican, with Bernini seated beside her in her carriage. By this gesture she immediately made plain to the populace wherein her chief interests and sympathies lay. Two days later she made a formal entry into the City dressed as an Amazon astride a white horse. Her reception in Rome was tumultuous. The Pope saw in her conversion what his successors saw in the faith of the exiled Stuarts, prospects of a united Christendom at last. The very spirit of Baroque extravagance and paradox seems somehow to have injected itself into Christina's nordic blood. She could do nothing calmly or conventionally. Though brought up as a man and accustomed to spartan conditions, she revelled in luxury and ceremony. A miracle of learning, Christina was as silly as a courtesan.

Her love for the arts was however passionate and sincere, and during her periodic residences in Rome her influence was both beneficial and widely felt. Bernini, who was not given to flattery, avowed that her knowledge of art exceeded that of most artists. Her return to Rome in 1658—she had had to leave for a while owing to lack of money and debts—resulted in shows, theatricals and opera in her honour, all of which productions had their due effect upon the output of architecture and sculpture. She employed the best Italian singers, whom she made world famous in her service, and appointed Alessandro Scarlatti her chapel master before he was twenty. Her affection for Bernini was very touching. She visited and comforted him on his deathbed and immediately after his funeral made Filippo Baldinucci write his biography. The consequence of her improvident patronage was a recrudescence of debts. At one moment she was reduced to pawning her clothes. After a visit to Sweden, where she was by no means welcome, she was back in Rome again in 1662 for another four years which were perhaps the happiest of her strange life. Now she was adding to her library in the Palazzo Riario, giving brilliant receptions and, because of her quixotic generosity to expatriate recusants from the northern countries, rising high in the favour of Alexander VII. Indeed she was never long in his or his successors' disfavour, and on a final return to Rome in 1668 was greeted by illuminations and fireworks and a public banquet at which the teetotal Clement IX toasted her in red lemonade. Henceforth she settled in the capital of her choice, and became the very cynosure of the cultured and artistic. As she told Bishop Burnet towards the end of her chequered career, she had grown to be one of the monuments of Rome.

3. Early Manifestations of Roman Baroque

PAINTING: THE CARACCI (fl. 1595–1609),
CARAVAGGIO (1573–1609) AND CORTONA (1596–1669)

By the end of the sixteenth century the Florentine and Venetian schools were spent forces. In Rome a disintegrating group of decorative painters was eking out a feeble Mannerist technique. In Bologna on the other hand a school was flourishing. This archiepiscopal city was now part of the Papal States, with a University which had produced some of the leading savants of the century, among whom Gregory XIII, Boncompagni (1572–85), may be included.[1] On the whole the Bolognese painters were intellectual in their approach to art. They did not exploit aesthetic ideals like the Florentines nor were they great colourists like the Venetians. So at a time when the Church, tired of the humanism and romantic antiquarianism of Bramante and Raphael and no longer in accord with the spiritual uncertainties expressed by Michelangelo's art, was seeking a more prosaic manner of decorating sacred edifices, the Bolognese painters were deemed appropriate instruments. In 1595 the Caracci family came to Rome from Bologna. In 1600 they began their great work for young Cardinal Odoardo Farnese on the ceiling of the Palazzo Farnese gallery. In spite of the ecclesiastical dignity of their patron the subjects of their paintings were frankly and very freely profane. In short, the loves of the gods was the theme which was expounded here and there in unashamedly erotic fashion.

The Farnese ceiling (*34*) marks a departure from the customary

---

[1] Gregory XV, Ludovisi (1621–23), the patron of his compatriot Domenichino, was also a Professor of Bologna University. Neither Gregory XIII nor Gregory XV was of aristocratic birth.

32   *Bust of Pope Innocent X, in the Palazzo Doria, Rome*
G. L. Bernini, sculptor

33   *S. Maria Maggiore, Rome: the Cappella Paolina (1611)*
Flaminio Ponzio, architect

34   *Palazzo Farnese, Rome. The Triumph of Bacchus and Ariadne: a panel in the Gallery Ceiling by the Caracci (c. 1600)*

35   *Villa Ludovisi, Rome. Detail of the Aurora Ceiling by Guercino (1591–1666)*

ways of late sixteenth-century decoration and is the first clear indication that Mannerism is on the wane. It was almost entirely the conception of Annibale Caracci's mind, and was executed by him with the assistance of his brother Agostino and his cousin Ludovico. Such a concerted enterprise had not been put in hand since Raphael's team worked on the Villa Farnesina eighty years or so before. The Caracci were fully aware of this fact, and their purpose was deliberately revivalist, being an attempt to combine features borrowed from Raphael's Loggie and Michelangelo's Sistine Chapel ceiling, without, however, reflecting either the serenity of Raphael or the turbulence of Michelangelo. Furthermore they dared to emulate the brilliance of Venetian colouring. In effect the ceiling showed a new respect for and understanding of the past. The Caracci had given new life to old rules and had promoted the rise of landscape painting by means of a more purposeful interpretation of nature than is found in any works of their contemporaries in Bologna. Moreover in the ambitious undertaking Annibale enlisted the co-operation of a number of young painters who were thereby permanently influenced by his teaching. Domenichino, his compatriot, produced in certain sections of the ceiling the first classical landscapes on a large scale. These still tentative efforts are none the less characteristic of his mature silvery tones, and are indicative of what he was to produce in the future. Guido Reni, also from Bologna, and Giovanni Lanfranco from Parma, both came to Rome for the same purpose. Their respective contributions to the ceiling are not perhaps so easily recognizable.

Yet the Farnese ceiling was not a Baroque work nor did its segregated compartments and isolated units have much influence upon Baroque composition. Rather it was one of the sources of that academic cross-current which was to run hither and thither throughout the seventeenth century, not necessarily in opposition but usually parallel to, even at times meeting and threading a way with the Baroque. In painting Ludovico Caracci, the most prolific of the family, became the leader of this group (Annibale died in 1609) to which Domenichino, Poussin and Claude belonged. In sculpture

Duquesnoy and Algardi, frankly hostile to the flamboyance of Bernini, of whose successes they were understandably jealous, remained in fairly consistent opposition to the Baroque movement. In architecture Domenico Fontana, Soria and the Genoese Bianco of the early seventeenth and Galilei and Fuga (whose styles were composite) of the eighteenth century never entirely lost sight of, if they sometimes strayed from, the path that was to lead to the Neoclassical field of Winckelmann. For influences upon Baroque painting other sources than the Farnese Palace ceiling must be looked for.

Five years before the Caracci moved to Rome a far more turbulent spirit had arrived who was to dispel the last vestiges of Mannerism. About the year 1590 Caravaggio made his first appearance in the City. He had been born in Lombardy in 1573 shortly after the youngest of the Caracci. This man with large questioning, dreamy eyes and a sulky mouth, was also a man of consuming passions which found vent in unrestrainable violence and criminal actions. He was possessed by what has been called *tristezza mortale*, an ineradicable melancholy, the isolating destiny of that genius which possessed Michelangelo. A deliberate realism is what distinguished his painting from the artificiality of the Mannerists; but it did not at all offer what the Papacy of the Late Counter-reformation was looking for. On the contrary, it caused much scandal and opposition. For Caravaggio's technique was something defiantly new. He revolted sharply against the prevailing, and obsequious, reverence for the established masters. Bellori[1] quotes him as dismissing with the angry contempt of youth the statues of Phidias and Glicon (which he can have known only from casts) while pointing to passers-by in the street as the right models for a contemporary artist. When he had occasion to paint an angel he would hail from the wayside some urchin to whose shoulders he attached with wax an old pair of wings kept in his studio for the purpose. His madonnas and saints were solid human flesh and blood found in the alleys and backwash of life. He spurned affected stances and etherialized expressions, preferring the natural gestures of commonplace models and the signs of joy or sorrow he saw stamped

[1] G. P. Bellori, *Vite de' Pittori, scultori et architetti*, 1672.

on the faces of his vulgar companions. His St. Matthew writing the Gospel (*39*), commissioned for the Contarelli Chapel in S. Luigi dei Francesi, did not look like the conventional conception of an Evangelist. Instead he was made to appear a bald, middle-aged peasant, sitting cross-legged, with feet, none too clean, in the fore-front of the picture, while a directing angel nestled beside him in a most irreverent, because intimate attitude. The picture had to be removed and the artist was made to do another. Furthermore Caravaggio's method of laying on paint was entirely novel. His contrasting lights and shadows, his luminous, sparkling bodies in metallic and marmoreal tones against sombre backgrounds were intended to appeal to the common man whose sense of the dramatic was more strongly developed than any other. In short Caravaggio's outlook was democratic, slightly anti-clerical, and therefore by no means welcome in Vatican circles. Friedlaender[1] has admirably summarized his brand of realism as "not so much detailed accuracy in rendering the natural object as a bringing of the object—the supernatural included—near to the spectator, almost to the degree of physical tangibility". Caravaggio's approach to the divine was, then, through the physical touch, by way of the senses, which is as good a way as any other. It is a mistake to assume that this sensualist who revelled in low life was merely a naturalist. It is more correct to call him a mystic of the down-to-earth sort. He was somewhat like St. Philip Neri whose direct, everyday approach to religion and whose adaptation to hymnology of well-known madrigal tunes find an echo in Caravaggio's own art. Moreover the enormous number of Caravaggio's commissions for altar-pieces suggests that the humbler clergy saw in him a realist of deep spiritual conviction with a very special gift of religious interpretation.

The younger generation of painters acclaimed him. They were inspired by his faithful interpretation of nature, by his popular bistro scenes and his dramatic effects. And although Caravaggio established no school in his lifetime his posthumous influence spread like Michelangelo's, only in lesser degree, all over Europe so that his

[1] Walter Friedlaender, *Caravaggio Studies*, 1955.

imitators became known as the *naturalisti*. Upon Spanish seventeenth-century painters—particularly Zurbarán—he had more influence than any other foreigner, not only in his handling of light and shade but in his revolutionary conception of the Godhead, saints and bishops.

Great therefore was the impact of Caravaggio not only on the Baroque painters but also on sculptors who learnt from him to invest the human form with a new dimension of plasticity and to depict it with a realism which had for too long been discounted by the Mannerists as something unrefined and ignoble. Nevertheless his rejection of tradition, healthy and inspiriting up to a point, could not be accepted wholeheartedly by his older contemporaries, who continued to hark back to the recent centuries for their sources of inspiration and even further back to the Ancients for their methods of composition.

In no important artist of the early Roman Baroque is the traditional spirit more steadfast than in Pietro da Cortona. In him we have the knot which ties Baroque architecture to the great Venetian painters of the sixteenth century just as in Bernini we have the link with the sculpture of Michelangelo. The one was essentially a painter, the other a sculptor. Each of them was also a great architect who through his primary medium helped to direct architecture into a new shape. In other words the style of Baroque architecture was anticipated as much in the background buildings found in the huge canvases of Veronese and Tintoretto as in the Laurenziana or the sculptural wall surfaces of the Medici Chapel.

It is well perhaps to reflect that Baroque painters were seldom more than slightly concerned with problems of form, harmony or style, which are abstractions now too arbitrarily read into their works by modern art historians. They were first of all concerned with the subject set before them, since their productions were chiefly judged by their contemporaries by the fidelity with which the history of a particular saint or martyr was represented. After that they busied themselves with the sentiment behind their paintings, and wondered whether it adequately fulfilled a didactic purpose. Only lastly did they worry whether their works would stand comparison with the masterpieces of those predecessors they happened most to revere. In rare cases did they self-consciously aim at affecting a particular style or directing the art of their day into some definable course. Lanfranco in decorating the dome of S. Andrea della Valle in 1621–25 doubtless kept somewhere at the back of his mind the high standard set by Correggio a hundred years previously in the Cathedral at Parma.[1] He naturally wished to emulate, even to improve upon him, and if there was a quality he tried to copy it was probably the sentiment of "tenderness" in Correggio which his generation especially admired. Lanfranco's "Assumption" was the first great Baroque painting in the monumental style, and it is among the most beautiful. There he admirably resolved the problem set before him of filling a large concave expanse with innumerable figures bound together in a dappled ocean of luminosity, supposedly emanating from the figure of Christ on the inner lantern but in reality from rays of daylight through apertures in the sides. Round the rim of the open eye, stucco foliage was so arranged to throw shadows over the first row of figures on the dome. Lanfranco thus initiated those decorative tricks of which Correggio knew nothing and to which he would probably not have condescended. Thereafter they became the stock in trade of Baroque artists in a determination to achieve startling effects.

Lanfranco's "Assumption" on the dome of S. Andrea, Guido Reni's "Phoebus and the Hours preceded by Aurora" in the garden house of the Palazzo Rospigliosi—a return from the Caravaggesque influence to that of antique sculpture—and Guercino's "Aurora" (*35*) in the Casino Ludovisi—that intimate echo of a Venetian ceiling assembly in predominating blue, yellow and grey—are three early Baroque masterpieces of painting in Rome. These works were meant to be merely decorative adjuncts subordinate to their background. They were not positively assertive and did not aim at overwhelming the architecture of their environment. On the other

---

[1] Correggio's painted cupola (1526) was the first large space to be covered without subdivisions.

hand the great fresco of the "Apotheosis of Urban VIII", with which Pietro da Cortona covered the saloon ceiling of the Palazzo Barberini between 1633 and 1639, can by no means be termed incidental (*36*). It floods the whole apartment with its presence. Everything sinks into insignificance before it. It marks a new stage in the evolution of Baroque architecture for which the painter was, consciously or unconsciously responsible. By this I do not mean that Cortona was literally drafting upon the ceiling the experiments of what he intended shortly to translate into stone. Nothing so obvious was in his mind, although the painted cornice and in particular the thick garlands upheld by naked figures are of that robust sort that was later to characterize his architectural style. It is in the composition of this great work that we find a parallel with his architecture. The Barberini "Apotheosis" is the first fresco on a huge scale made to embrace one untrammelled field. Unlike the Farnese Gallery ceiling the separate scenes enacted are not grouped within real compartments made of stucco. Even so the artist has built up his theme by a synthesis of groups. His very prominent painted cornice supported by emphatic brackets, forms a criss-cross of horizontals and verticals. Whereas previous ceiling painters had made use of existing architectural features between which they painted the distant sky Cortona has feigned an architecture for the same purpose. Thus he has deliberately created a limitation in order to overcome it and induce a victorious sense of height and boundless space.

Pietro da Cortona belongs to the generation of Bernini and Borromini, being older than the first by two years and the last by three. By the time he began work upon the Barberini ceiling he was nearly forty, and had of course previously painted much, and even built a little. Already his frescoes in S. Bibiana had made him the father of a new form of large-scale decorative painting which lasted for two generations. As a vivid colourist in the tradition of the Venetians he was unexcelled. In making brilliant lemon yellows and sky blues vibrate against pearl, mauve or lilac grounds he was only matched by Solimena and Tiepolo a century later. In 1645 John Evelyn recorded that he was held to be the best painter then in Rome. The

Barberini ceiling took five years to complete and during the period Cardinal Francesco Barberini commissioned him to rebuild the church of S. Luca over the ancient underground church of S. Martina. The two works followed a parallel course. The Church of S. Luca is the artist's unhindered interpretation of the Baroque (37). The beauty of Cortona's style is here seen in a massive unity of plastic forms rather than a concatenation of sculptural reliefs. Its difference to the style of Bernini's work is manifest. There are none of the great sculptor's tapestry effects, none of his animal or vegetable motifs introduced in the detail. Instead a painter's harmony and sobriety of tone prevail throughout. Paradoxically enough no polychrome materials are used in the interior of the church, which is uniformly and almost glacially white. Cortona the brilliant colourist has purposely withheld an element he considered unsuitable to archi- tecture, an element which the Baroque architects who were not painters seemed to find indispensable.[1] The artist has achieved his effects by a studied juxtaposition of solids and voids and above all by contrasts of lights and shadows which flicker over the columns and niches of the nave and engender a liveliness wholly alien to Counter- reformation buildings. The impression gained is that there are no boundaries to the interior, whereas in reality the space is not large, and that the wall surfaces are a flow of gentle undulations. The rich harmony resulting from the dissonant parts of S. Luca has, like the orchestral accompaniments of Monteverdi, the power of provoking deep meditation.

The remarkably pictorial element of S. Luca, wherein an agglomera- tion of masses is built up as in a vast decorative picture towards a focal feature (here of course inside and out it is the dome which predominates, for the equi-sized arms of this church form a Greek cross) is repeated in Cortona's two later Roman churches, S. Maria della Pace and S. Maria in Via Lata. The painter, although he complained that architecture never brought him luck and that his projects in this venture were too seldom adopted, could not keep

---

1 The architecture of A. Gherardi, who like Cortona was primarily a Baroque painter, is also monochrome.

away from it. S. Maria della Pace, with its wonderful play of convex façade and portico against a concave screen, like a stage backcloth gently swollen by a draught from the wings at the moment when the curtain is drawn up, invokes a gasp of wonder and a cry of joy from the fortunate person who comes upon it for the first time. It is all there is of Cortona's work, for the body of the church was here before him. We have difficulty in believing that the scene confronting us so full of movement is really made of hard travertine. S. Maria in Via Lata is a less dramatic but not less subtle composition (*43*). Upon its straight façade, which dutifully carries on the line of the Corso, the artist has brought about a feeling of plasticity by making the central arch of the upper order trespass upon the pediment—the very same conceit as that we saw in the end faces of the Triumphal Arch at Orange.[1] The arrangement provides a welcome form of relief to the severely vertical "Pantheon" spacing of the columns, duplicated upon both stages, like two strident chords struck one after the other. A comparable light relief is found in the apses and the barrel ceiling of the portico, which opens straight on to the street.

Cortona was not the first to build in the full Baroque style, although S. Luca is one of the earliest Roman churches wholly free from Mannerism. He was one of the great figures of the age and his influence upon his successors was profound. Not only was he the progenitor of seventeenth-century decorative painters on the monumental scale, men like G. B. Gaulli and Andrea Pozzo, who covered vast areas of Jesuit churches in Italy and Austria, but Le Brun and Verrio who followed suit in France and England. He steeped Baroque architecture in that pictorial element which is peculiar to the style. He indirectly taught later generations of architects, notably Juvara and Neumann, to assemble churches and palaces in planes and masses as though they were feigned buildings on canvas or fresco, which nevertheless aspired to some co-ordinating feature outside an area vouchsafed by space and time.

[1] This unconventional conceit is found in the loggia to the Vestibulum of Diocletian's Palace at Spalato in a repetitive form. Vignola had adopted the theme in his Chapel at Bomarzo.

36 *Detail of Pietro da Cortona's ceiling: the Apotheosis of Pope Urban VIII*
(1633–9) in the Palazzo Barberini, Rome

37 *S. Luca, Rome (1634)*
Pietro da Cortona, architect

38 *SS. Vincenzio ed Anastasio, Rome (1650)*
Martino Longhi, architect

39   *St. Matthew writing the Gospel, commissioned for S. Luigi dei Francesi, Rome, by Caravaggio (1569–1609) (formerly in Berlin; now destroyed)*

FAÇADES

Eugenio D'Ors has claimed that the Baroque is only manifest in façades.[1] This over-simplification has in it a grain of truth because the Baroque aims at making a stupendous impact upon first sight often to the neglect of later impressions. There are innumerable mediocre seventeenth-century buildings where only the façade is in the Baroque style, the body being in a tame and nondescript classical. The designer simply concentrated on the entrance and left the rest to its own devices.[2] This negligence is in absolute contrast to Cortona's method which was to knit façade to body in a massive whole. He was perhaps exceptional in this respect. Certainly no Baroque architect scamped the façade, whereas in mediaeval and Renaissance Italy it was often overlooked altogether. Thus Siena Cathedral lacked a façade until the nineteenth century; S. Lorenzo in Florence remains without one to this day.

The Mediaeval age concentrated primarily on the soul of man: the Renaissance on man's physical relation to the universe in terms of geometrical proportion. Both ages were so addicted to the truth that a façade must faithfully interpret what went on behind it or be absent. The embellishment of the inside of a house of God, whether for spiritual or aesthetic reasons, was what mattered and by the time this was completed funds had often run out and there was nothing left to spend on the front. But the Baroque age which disregarded the truth if it meant a conflict with its objective, often imposed façades which bore no relation whatever to the interior. Thus in Sicily we come across ornate church-façades towering magnificently into the sky, which from a frontal view are most impressive but, when seen from the side with only a meagre attachment to one-third of their height, look deceptive and ridiculous. Enormous windows will often illuminate a blank wall with nothing behind it. On the ground floor vast portals may give entry to an

---

[1] Eugenio D'Ors, *Du Baroque*, 1935.
[2] I am not referring to those many Renaissance churches to which a Baroque façade was added.

exiguous cabin in which the only light is derived from a slit or two in the clerestory. The interior of this kind of church is like a prehistoric cave dwelling, or the Treasury of Atreus with its monumental entrance to a dark chamber carved out of the rock, where a single eye in the roof casts down a lurid pinpoint of light. In church-building sacrifice of convenience to appearance is all very well. Men do not have to live in churches where lack of light and an outdoor view may even be desirable. But in domestic dwellings these and kindred amenities are universally appreciated. The Palace built by Paul V opposite the Papal Palace at Avignon, for instance, so far follows the principle of the Baroque church façade that not only is the top third of the front without any rear to it but the middle third has no windows at all (*41*). The whole front is purely a screen, extremely bold and beautiful, but sadly unpractical and quite unfit for habitation. Hardly more satisfactory is that room in the Municipio at Padua which has a Baroque monument of elegant proportions completely blocking the outside of the window.

Until about 1630 the severe Counter-reformation façade still prevailed in Rome. It had changed little from the Gesù archetype. Soria's front added to Maderna's S. Maria della Vittoria in 1626 is very typical, a tight, compressed composition of two stages, a smaller over a larger, with the ubiquitous scrolls uniting the one to the other above the aisle bays. There is nothing sinuous or flowing here, nothing pictorial. All is staid and heavy. Few concessions are made to surface effect by the prim pilasters of the two orders. But then Soria, who lived until 1651, never, as I have already indicated, succumbed to the Baroque. Variants of this type of façade persisted with little apparent development. Sometimes the upper stage was made as wide as the lower (as at S. Bartolommeo dell'Isola), sometimes flanked by twin towers (as at the Trinità dei Monti). After 1630 greater attention was paid to the play of light and shadow upon surfaces. As early as 1603 Maderna had treated the lower stage of S. Susanna with engaged columns instead of the customary pilasters, which he limited to the angles. The result is certainly striking, as Evelyn was quick to notice for he called it "the most ravishing front" (40). On a church façade this treatment was a deliberate innovation, tending to give a sense of solidity and strong relief essentially sculptural. With Carlo Rainaldi the treatment developed at S. Maria in Campitelli into fully disengaged columns. The theme was tremendously emphasized by Martino Longhi in the middle of the century on the façade of SS. Vicenzo ed Anastasio which, in consequence of the phalanx of advancing pediments that the columns support, becomes highly sculptural, three-dimensional, sumptuous and solid (38). Indeed the smooth white columns standing out against a dark background like a row of Caravaggesque nudes have a luminous quality which is more usually experienced in painting than in architecture.[1] When the High Baroque is in full swing church façades cease to have an upper stage narrow like a tower; on the contrary both stages are composed within a regular rectangle. The undulating front which first appeared in S. Luca is the order of the day, whether it be seen in the narrow elevation of S. Marcello or the monumental spread of S. Agnese in Agone.

The design of the Roman palace on the other hand altered remarkably little throughout the seventeenth century from what it had been under the Counter-reformation Popes, except in a general tendency to magnify the rank of the owner; with the villa the setting in relation to the garden became increasingly important. The chief change noticeable in the palace façade is the abandonment of superimposed orders on account of the ugly angles resulting when viewed in profile. Since this inconvenience does not arise in a courtyard where no end profiles are visible the double order is still sometimes found there. The solution resorted to on the façade was to embrace the principal storeys within a giant order as Michelangelo had been the first to do in the palaces of the Capitol. A new decorative device much in evidence is the cartouche for the proud display of princely arms and quarterings, which makes an appearance over the entrance portal and sometimes breasts the skyline, dominating the statues ranged on either side of it. Since a central feature requires as much emphasis as

[1] They have been likened by Victor L. Tapié (Baroque et Classicisme, 1957) to a range of powerful organ pipes.

possible, a cluster around the entrance is now usual, consisting of perhaps two lesser doorways (or two pedimented windows) on either side the middle one, all within a single order under a balustrade or a balcony. Thus the rest of the façade may be entirely eclipsed by this central feature. For a Baroque elevation either implies a single motif expanding and even ultimately exploding over the whole surface or else every part being kept entirely subordinate to the whole. In Renaissance palace façades neither alternative was usual. Each storey and each bay of a storey was in itself an independent and repetitive entity, no one being more or less important than its fellow. The whole was formed out of lesser separate parts. This formula is observable in Bramante's Palazzo Cancelleria, even in Palladio's Palazzo Porto Barbarano in Vicenza. Slice off a bay, and the composition is not thereby made meaningless. Indeed the Palazzo Porto Breganze by Palladio has only two bays left and is still an object of veneration. If a Baroque palace were to lose one bay—which in itself might be meaningless—the balance of the whole would be irremediably upset and incalculable mischief would ensue.

The consequence is that a Baroque façade appears to change from every different viewpoint. A Renaissance façade remains the same; or rather, to be appreciated properly it must to be viewed frontally. From an angle it merely becomes distorted like the film on a cinema screen seen from seats at the extreme sides of the auditorium. A Baroque façade viewed from the sides looks different, but not out of perspective. For its set purpose is to convey an impression of endless movement, a constant striving to become something new and different. It is like the water in Pope Urban VIII's sonnet to the Fountain which:

> *Si d'uno in altro moto si trasforma,*
> *Che, sebben nel cristal mobile immota*
> *Sua sembianza abbia il fonte, l'occhio crede*
> *Ch'ognor si cangi in varia e nuova forma.*

Hence the frequent metaphor that a Baroque façade is a Renaissance façade plunged in moving water. It does not, however, absolutely meet the case in spite of the Baroque age's quite exotic love of fountains. A reflection in fountain water implies jagged, broken outlines and not the cheerful flow of contours caused by a gently rippling pool or purling stream. For Baroque palaces are as cheerful as Renaissance ones are melancholy. Henry James hit upon this discovery when in describing the Palazzo Barberini he remarked that "its only fault . . . is perhaps the large brightness of its face, a note almost of modern gaiety in its complexion and its open approaches ; the note repeated . . . in all the heterogeneous pleasantness and poetry of rearward, sideward views—blue, Claude-like distant things and brown, yellow, amusing near ones . . . unsuspected revelations and possessions, waste Barberini courts, terraces, treasures of space . . .".[1] The water simile is more applicable to the Rococo, which signifies the jerk forward, the halt, the retreat and the general breathless pace as of a man in bewilderment, not knowing whether he is coming or going. The Baroque was so sure of its appearance from every angle that it frequently sited buildings obliquely. S. Croce in Gerusalemme, for example, is approached at an angle by the straight road descending from the Lateran, so that the full façade gradually unfolds itself to the view like the petals of a rose before the rising sun. The Fontana Paolina is likewise first seen set askew to the road which ascends towards it from S. Pietro in Montorio. A regard for surroundings and a splendid sense of occasion distinguish the Baroque from previous ages. The setting of the Salute Church, at the point where the Grand Canal flows into the Venetian lagoon, and that of the Monastery at Melk, on the prow of a rock which meets the surging waters of the Danube, take supreme advantage of the dramatic sites provided by nature. Moreover both these great monuments may be seen today in exactly the same environment which their creators chose for them.

BERNINI (1598–1680) AND THE INFLUENCE OF SCULPTURE

Carlo Maderna (1556–1629) was to become the first recognizably Baroque architect in spite of the fact that his working life started

[1] Henry James, *William Wetmore Story and His Friends*, 1903.

at the height of the Counter-reformation in the reign of Sixtus V. He was Domenico Fontana's nephew and came from Lake Lugano. By training he was a sculptor. He began by helping his uncle on many monuments as well as the great catafalque for Pope Sixtus. At first he imitated him in spirit and form. On Fontana's disgrace and departure from Rome after the Pope's death the nephew found himself obliged to continue several of his uncle's unfinished buildings. Gradually he was transmuted into an architect. His heyday was the reign of Paul V before the brighter stars of a later generation of architects had arisen in the firmament, and his greatest work was the completion of the nave and the addition of the façade of St. Peter's. Here Maderna was hampered by the plans of his predecessors and the dictates of the Curia. For liturgical, not aesthetic reasons, he was obliged to discard the original Greek cross plan and substitute the Latin cross with its long nave, greatly to the detriment of Michelangelo's dome which in consequence was hidden from all but distant views. His façade is not distinguished but it is only fair to him to remember that he wished to build towers at either end of it. These would have reduced the great bulk of the façade—it is too long for its height—and at least have made it a more fitting base for the dome as seen from the Ponte S. Angelo and the various heights of the City. But Maderna's intentions were no more realized than Bernini's towers, which were actually begun at a slightly later date, were completed.

Maderna's innovations at St. Peter's were the choice of a beautiful travertine of delicate golden tint and the re-use, after half a century, of free standing columns of the colossal order for the façade. The work was not begun till 1607, which was four years after he had first experimented with columns on the lower stage of S. Susanna. His idea was no doubt to minimize that squatness of St. Peter's façade to which I have referred and which the addition of the two towers would have dispelled altogether. As it is the tall columns are meant to induce a vertical effect in contradistinction to the horizontal motif of the too commonly reproduced Gesù front.

In the Palazzo Mattei, Maderna has made a distinct breakaway from Fontana's severe domestic style of building. He has animated his masses, particularly in the courtyard, by means of deep moulded reliefs, busts and epigraphs, thus introducing rich decorative patterns which are a novelty. At the entrance to his stairs he has provided a perspective arch to simulate a greater width than they in fact possess. Maderna's death in 1629 marks the end of the experimental Baroque phase and leaves the way clear for the greatest artist of the century to come to the fore. With the dawn of the 1630s Bernini succeeded him as papal architect.

When Bernini was appointed Architect to the Fabric of St. Peter's he was thirty-one years old. Of medium height and spare build he had the fierce profile and the fierce temperament of an eagle. He was a man of immense versatility and learning in the true Renaissance tradition. He consistently impressed upon his pupils the artist's need for a universal culture and always upheld Poussin because of his superior erudition. Undoubtedly his learning was one of the qualities which attracted him to Urban VIII, whose accession in 1623 had assured the young man's future, just as his Jesuit upbringing had earlier recommended him to Gregory XV. The words of the splendid Pontiff at the sculptor's first audience are well known: "It is a piece of good luck for you, Cavaliere, to see Cardinal Maffeo Barberini Pope, but far greater is our good fortune that the lifetime of Cavaliere Bernini should fall within our pontificate"—a generous speech borne out by the chance of an unusually long reign. At the end of it Bernini's success and fame were so established that the set-back under the succeeding Pope could only be temporary. Baldinucci, his first biographer, states that Urban, after the initial compliment, then urged him to practise painting and architecture as well as sculpture, which recalls Julius II forcing Michelangelo to adopt an art that was not his natural medium by commissioning the reluctant genius to paint the Sistine Chapel ceiling. And the relations between Urban and Bernini were not altogether dissimilar to those between Julius and Michelangelo. The two men reached an intimacy seldom possible between a Pope and an artist. Urban frequently honoured Bernini with visits to his studio, whither on one occasion he was accompanied by a cavalcade of sixty cardinals amid the applause of the city populace. If these visits were not quite as informal as those made by Julius, who, wearing his pontifical robes, would perch upon a step-ladder chatting to Michelangelo in overalls with his beard matted with paint, it was due to a greater conception of the dignity befitting the Vicar of Christ in the Baroque age. Their relations too were smoother, for the seventeenth-century Pope and artist, although made in the same titanic mould, lacked that quantity of gunpowder in the disposition of their sixteenth-century counterparts. Bernini may from the first have foreseen in the association a similar promising outcome, for Michelangelo was the artist he admired above all others. Chantelou[1], who accompanied him on his abortive visit to Paris in 1665, records that the name of no artist was more frequently on Bernini's lips and there was no one he more earnestly wished to emulate; that since Michelangelo never did portrait busts, he, Bernini, was determined to excel in this respect. His loyalty to the classical idiom and tradition was second only to that of Michelangelo. He constantly taught his students that it was of greater importance to study and copy the antique than to draw direct from nature. This may be surprising to those who have not given much thought to the motives of the artist whose name is more frequently associated with the Baroque than any other.

The still common misunderstanding that Bernini's art is the very antithesis to the antique is of course traceable to the men of the Neo-classical revival. Winckelmann[2] had not a good word for Bernini, seeing in his work more than the negation of the classical concept, which he considered Michelangelo had been the first to flaunt, and the positive exploitation of ugliness for its own sake. Bernini, he says, "has mistaken the reverse of beauty for beauty's self". He was utterly corrupted by the coarse and uncultivated. "He sought to dignify by exaggeration forms of the most ordinary kind." Herein lies a measure of truth which the author of the state-

---

[1] Paul Fréart de Chantelou, *Journal du Voyage en France du Cavalier Bernin*, 1930.

[2] J. Winckelmann, *History of Ancient Art*, vol. 1, trs. 1881.

40 *S. Susanna, Rome: detail of the façade (1603)*
Carlo Maderna, architect

41 *Palais de la Monnaie, or Palace of Pope Paul V (1605–21), Avignon*

42 *Bust of Cardinal Scipione Borghese in the Casino Borghese, Rome*
G. L. Bernini, sculptor

ment hardly meant to be flattering. What Winckelmann, who sought to elevate art so that it should reflect again the ancient ideals of the everlasting harmonies, could not condone was Bernini's interpretation of common human qualities. What in his opinion was a degradation of art was in Bernini's an elevation of the human spirit. Bernini wanted to make of art a truth, Winckelmann a fiction. "His figures", Winckelmann continued, "are those of vulgar people who have suddenly met with good fortune"; and if he had in mind the busts of Cardinal Scipione Borghese (*42*) and Constanza Bonarelli he was right, for the one had risen to great wealth and position through nepotism, the other to the uncertain luxury of a famous artist's mistress from humble origins. Mr. Thomas Baker too has the insolent swagger of the bounder. But what masterpieces of interpretation these three works are, for the very reason that Winckelmann deplored. Although a subject is a parvenu, a kept woman or a cad, the image may be a work of art. Bishop Berkeley,[1] who was not an art historian but an eclectic with a mind open to religion, science and art alike and who lived at a time when the Baroque was still the accepted European style, saw Bernini's work in another light. "I must not forget", he wrote after a visit to the Borghese Casino in 1717, "three statues of Bernini in these apartments, that raise my idea of that modern statuary almost to an equality with the famous ancients— Apollo and Daphne, Aeneas with Anchises on his shoulders, David going to fling the stone at Goliath."

These three groups which Bishop Berkeley singled out for praise were all done by Bernini before 1630 when he was exclusively a statuary. On his coming to Rome as a youth in the second decade of the century sculpture had been neglected for over fifty years. When statues were needed for the Paoline Chapel in S. Maria Maggiore foreign artists had to be called upon from Milan, France and Flanders. Like Michelangelo Bernini found himself without any serious rivals. Francesco Mochi, nineteen years his senior, was feebly striving to free himself from Mannerist stiffness.[2] But rivals in

---

[1] Bishop G. Berkeley, *Journal of a Tour in Italy*, 1717, 1718.
[2] Mochi's best known work is the figure of St. Veronica on one of the four

sculpture arose. The two most formidable, whose studios were in much demand, were François Duquesnoy and Alessandro Algardi. Duquesnoy was a Fleming who resolutely refused to identify himself with Bernini's Baroque. He was more obsessed by the Antique than any of the seventeenth-century sculptors and his many funerary monuments and religious subjects in Roman churches have a purely classical serenity, of which his S. Susanna in S. Maria di Loreto is an example. Algardi came to Rome from Bologna in 1625 and began to earn a living as a restorer of antique sculpture. Bellori, who disliked Bernini, called Algardi "the most intelligent sculptor of his time . . . by whose hands the spirit of marble was revived". Whereas Bernini's sculpture was impetuous and centrifugal, Algardi's was realistic and precise; as a boy he had been trained to be a goldsmith. He was a splendid portraitist—his Donna Olimpia Pamphili is a masterpiece—with a ready gift of narrative. Yet his penetrating mind was fettered by a slavery to detail. Algardi was essentially a sculptor of likenesses and when he turned to architecture and built the Villa Pamphili he allowed himself to be bogged in a morass of decorative relief which he adopted from Hadrian's Villa. He belonged to the academic school of Domenichino and Poussin which ran counter to the Baroque.

By intensive study of the Ancients and of Michelangelo the young Bernini sought to revive Roman sculpture from its fifty years' lethargy. His Apollo (*26*) and Daphne and Aeneas and Anchises were inspired by both sources in subject and in certain particulars. The themes are Virgilian. The head of Apollo is taken from the Apollo Belvedere (*27*): and the pose (as Wittkower[1] has pointed out) and even the slightly insipid head of Aeneas from Michelangelo's Christ in S. Maria sopra Minerva. But to these works has been added a new element, unknown to the classical Greeks, not more than sensed by the Pergamenes and not even used by Michelangelo. That element

piers of St. Peter's. It is certainly full of movement. When Bernini asked him whence came the wind that made her draperies blow about so violently, the reply was "From the fissures in the dome caused by your antics in digging the foundations of the Baldacchino."

[1] R. Wittkower, *Gian Lorenzo Bernini, Sculptor of the Roman Baroque*, 1955.

is action. Bernini's David exemplifies this element to the utmost. There is little doubt that in conceiving the statue Bernini was mindful of Michelangelo's masterpiece and fired by ambition to emulate it. The different approach to the same subject by the two artists is most marked. Where Michelangelo's David stands victorious and brooding after having slain Goliath, Bernini's David is concentrated upon the desperate act of slaughter. Every muscle in the young body is taut, every fibre is in play at this supreme moment when salvation or death hang in the balance. The boy hero's grim, set face with lips compressed, is concentrated in an agony of purpose upon an object out of sight. We are made instinctively to turn from David and look away for Goliath in the distance. We become participants with Bernini in the awful scene of retribution which is on the brink of happening. Such tension can by its very nature only be momentary. The sculptor has in fact seized the passing of a split second. Nothing like Bernini's David had been achieved in marble before. No wonder Winckelmann was shocked by so much unseemly movement. The Pergamenes, it is true, had carved men in action. The Discobolos is such a statue, with its bent form and arm drawn back about to throw the discus; but the process is calm and eternal. The Discobolos is a "foster-child of Silence and slow Time", and like the figures on Keats's Grecian Urn something that has been arrested for ever in a state of inactive activity. Michelangelo's solitary figures preserved the Greek quality. They remained apart, transfixed in savage silence, contemplating eternity. Only Giovanni da Bologna of the Italian Mannerist sculptors had in him the germ of that emotional vehemence and dynamic movement which so stirred in Bernini that he transmitted it into the whole of Baroque sculpture and architecture.

And where Bernini does not mean to convey movement by action he often cunningly suggests it in a rippling suppleness of human flesh and integument. We have merely to look where the cruel fingers of his Pluto press firmly into the soft flank of Proserpine, where the oceanic flow of his Neptune's hair, beard and even eyebrows is pulled from the scalp of the angry god's head like seaweed from a rock. Only

Rubens in a different medium had hitherto portrayed the same tense and quivering mobility of the flesh. To render it in marble was a *tour-de-force*. At times Bernini overreached himself, for there are limits to the potentialities of marble. The texture of this hard, unyielding material does not always lend itself to representing nature's more ethereal components. In endeavouring to exploit his scientific mastery over form he sometimes demanded more than marble was capable of yielding. Certainly his followers, with less understanding of the material and less genius than his, were apt to make fools of themselves. If Bernini barely gets away with the marble flames crackling under the gridiron of his St. Lawrence, Ercole Ferrata, in spite of much technical ability, is still less convincing in the shooting tongues of fire made to envelope his St. Agnes. The consequence was an insipidity to which Bernini himself occasionally fell victim. This weakness is no less apparent where he essays great suffering or grief. His languishing St. Sebastian and his weeping cherubs nauseate rather than move us to pity. Sometimes they will even move us to laughter.

In his determination to surpass Michelangelo with the portrait bust—where he succeeded past all belief—Bernini was well aware of the temerity of the task. He told young Nicholas Stone that he wanted to show the English how it could be done, which is why he attached so much importance to the safe arrival in London of his bust of Charles I. He asked the student with childlike eagerness whether it had suffered the slightest damage in transit, and how much it was admired by his countrymen. For "I conclude", he said, "that it is the impossible thing [*sic*] in the world to make a picture in stone naturally to resemble any person".[1] None the less this conviction did not prevent him from repeatedly making the attempt. Never before had a sculptor developed so intricate a technique in this regard. Chantelou gives a fascinating account of the manner in which he worked upon the bust of Louis XIV.[2] After taking innumerable sketches and then making clay models of the King playing tennis and

[1] Quoted by Stone in his Diary of 1638.
[2] See also R. Wittkower's *Bernini's Bust of Louis XIV*, 1951.

43 *S. Maria in Via Lata,*
Rome (1660)
Pietro da Cortona, architect

44 *The Scala Regia, Vati-*
can Palace (c. 1665)
G. L. Bernini, architect

45 *The Emperor Constantine (St. Peter's, Rome)*
G. L. Bernini, sculptor

46 *St. Peter's, Rome: part of the great Colonnade (begun 1667)*
G. L. Bernini, architect

47 *S. Maria della Vittoria, Rome: detail from the Cornaro Chapel (1644–7)*
G. L. Bernini, sculptor

presiding over meetings of his ministers, he obliged him to sit hourly on thirteen successive afternoons at precisely the same time of day so that the density of the light should be invariable. To denote majesty he purposely overemphasized certain features of the monarch's face, namely the aquiline nose, the bumps over the eyes— deeply shadowed to suggest colour—and the recession of the forehead. For, he explained, in the portrait bust a sculptor must sometimes mould what is not in nature in order to convey a natural impression, such as exaggerated depth round the eyes in order to represent pallor. He set Louis's head thrown back and made the lips slightly parted as though on the point of issuing a command. The smoke- like, almost evanescent, curls of the periwig and the swirl of the drapery from left to right of the body give the impression of a critical instant arrested in the haughty king's daily life, about to lead to some immediate action of far-reaching consequence.

In the Cornaro Chapel of S. Maria della Vittoria, Bernini (with the assistance of pupils) has deliberately made sculpture do the work of painting (47). On either side he has assembled members of the Cornaro family sitting as though in opera boxes, reading, discussing and watching the ecstasy of St. Teresa as though it were a scene on the stage, and not a profoundly sacred mystic experience.[1] The figures of the audience are in high relief before the *trompe-l'œil* background of a receding colonnade, which is half real, half sham architecture. Furthermore, coloured marbles have been introduced to set off the white robes of the family—mostly clerics—and to represent the sumptuous hangings and cushions draped over the ledge of each box. The theatrical effect is emphasized by borrowed light which from a concealed window is thrown down upon the Saint and attendant angel with his dart of divine love, and brilliantly reflected by the golden shafts (made of metal) representing heavenly fire. In the Cappella Raimondi in S. Pietro in Montorio Bernini had previously tried out this sculptural–architectural device to which a pictorial effect was lent by oblique and concealed lighting, without however

---

[1] *Si c'est ici l'amour divin,* remarked the cynical Président De Brosses, *je le connais.*

125

resort being had to any polychromatic decoration. The material is uniform white marble.

The quasi-architectural perspective background of the boxes in the Cornaro Chapel was the outcome of Bernini's skill as a theatrical designer and master of *trompe-l'œil*. This combination of talent was brought to a thrilling pitch in the production of his Comedy of Two Theatres at the Carnival of 1637 when a presentation of two scenes was given simultaneously by an ingenious method of reflecting mirrors. The audience was enchanted but disturbed to witness a counterfeit audience applauding another performance to the one enacted before their eyes. Illusionism was the favourite sport of the century. Upon the front of the Palazzo Barberini Bernini had contrived on the second floor a row of seven windows with archivolts and reveals so splayed that they induced a make-believe impression of leading to a balustraded colonnade. At this palace, which on Maderna's death Bernini in unhappy partnership with Borromini took over incomplete, his first essays at true architectural perspective are to be seen.

They found their ultimate fulfilment in the Scala Regia at the Vatican (*44*). Here, as Professor Pane[1] points out, Bernini perfected the technique of perspective illusion first experimented upon by Bramante at S. Satiro, Milan, and developed by Palladio in receding vistas in the Teatro Olimpico at Vicenza.[2] Neither of the last two architects however had to suit his effects to exigencies of site. Bernini's triumph was remarkable in that the site of his undertaking was exceptionally awkward. Because of the existing wall which connects the Cathedral with the Colonnade and to an abutting end of the Sala Regia, the space allowed was neither straight nor wide. Furthermore the ground did not rise evenly. As a result Bernini's long entrant corridor and stairs could not be properly aligned or evenly graded. Nevertheless by an almost superhuman dexterity he so arranged matters that a vista was preserved from end to end. The

[1] Roberto Pane, *Bernini architetto*, 1953.

[2] It is more than likely that Bernini derived the idea of a long tunnel-like passage from Borromini's perspective portico at the Palazzo Spada which had been finished in 1636.

long progressive ramp of the preliminary corridor with its arched and vaulted roof is evenly maintained until the stairs are reached. Thereupon the stairs are made to rise without a corresponding rise in the ceiling height. The right wall gradually closes in and the columns along it get smaller and smaller. Whereas the corridor could be lit by tall windows from the connecting wall on the south, light for the stairs had to be borrowed from above at strategic points and from one window at the extreme end of the long first flight. The simplicity of the architecture of the initial corridor, leading to the contrasting richness of the stair columns and coffered ceiling, was part of Bernini's express intention that the foreign visitor seeking an audience of the Pope should be increasingly awed by the prospect before him—the tremendous distance being accentuated by pools of light on the way up and a pinpoint of light at the far end. His trepidation on mounting was correspondingly changed to relief on the return journey by a reverse impression of foreshortening.

The Scala Regia and the great elliptical Colonnade, to which it is the corollary, by themselves put Bernini in the very forefront of the world's architects. The sheer technical achievement of both is the work of genius. Who else would have appreciated that to benefit from the vast scale of St. Peter's and to maintain a glimpse of Michelangelo's dome—which Paul V's Curia had done their best to minimize by insisting upon a Latin cross nave—a piazza must be set away from the main front, yet without appearing to be so? As it is, the space between the portico and piazza is about two-thirds the depth of the piazza. By the expansion instead of contraction of the connecting arms as they near the basilica the visitor in the piazza is deceived into supposing he is closer to the shadow of the entrance than he actually is. Again, Bernini purposely made his Colonnade lower than Maderna's portico in order to make the latter look higher than it is, its fault being that in proportion to the height of the façade it is too low.

This acutely developed sense of architectural perspective and this ability to delude, or rather delight, the eye, could only derive from a sculptor's understanding of the round. It was as if Bernini literally moulded his buildings with his own tactile fingers. The pulsing oval enclosed within the Colonnade's wide embracing arms, of which all the component parts are strictly classical, might have been carved out of the solid like the torso of some relaxed giant. We are constantly struck by this quality in Bernini's architecture and overcome by the difficulty of deciding at times when his work is architecture and when sculpture. It is this unresolved, irrational factor that has always infuriated his detractors. The subterfuges to which he resorted strike them as dishonest He sought to make materials play a part that from their very nature they, strictly speaking, could not play but which his genius could succeed in making them appear to play. Thus he often replaced conventional architectural members like entablatures, columns, jambs and plinths by figures, draperies, rocks and flowers, which might be composed of marble, stone, stucco or metal, whichever by its texture he found most sympathetic and most readily to hand. This mixing of materials is very apparent on his vast monuments in St. Peter's (*31*): also in that wonderful conceit in the Sala Ducale in the Vatican (*48*) where he made two rooms with only a narrow opening between appear to be one by means of flying *putti* holding back feigned heavy draperies and an escutcheon. He created an astounding beauty of movement, not out of what was, but out of what seemed to be.

The great Colonnade (*46*) and the Cathedra Petri inside the basilica were erected towards the end of his career: the Baldacchino over the bones of St. Peter was erected at the outset. It was his first attempt at architecture. It was begun in 1624 at the instigation of Urban VIII. When finished it was greeted by his contemporaries as a masterpiece. A century later that distinguished traveller from France, the Président De Brosses, regarded it as the finest work of its kind in the whole world. A little more than fifty years were to pass and Sir John Soane called it "a lasting reproach to his memory"; and some fifty years again after that Burckhardt was writing in the middle of the nineteenth century of "the dreadful baldacchino" which in 1913 Mr. Briggs complained "outrages our sober British taste". Now what is this astonishing object made out of the bronze beams of the Pantheon

48 *Arch of the Sala Ducale, Vatican, Rome*
G. L. Bernini, architect

49 *S. Maria della*
Piazza, Turin (1751):
interior of Cupola
B. Vittone, architect

50 *St. Peter's, Rome: detail of the Cathedra Petri (1667)*
G. L. Bernini, sculptor

portico and weighing 186,392 lbs that has aroused such conflicting opinions? Is it architecture? Or is it really sculpture after all? Can architecture be adorned with tasselled pelmets of bronze and assume the shape of a rustic arbour, having for support twisted stems entwined with vegetation? Bernini did not care so long as it suitably honoured the shrine of the first of the Apostles under the crossing, without impeding a through view of the basilica from the entrance to the apse. Above all it satisfied the prerequisites of the Church's desire for splendour and his own romantic notions. Now romanticism unrestrained by the discipline of classicism was eventually to mark the change from Baroque into Rococo, the constant into the unexpected. It was to end in the decline of that tradition which, albeit with interruptions, had flourished since ancient times, into a subsequent artificial revival of styles and then into the disappearance of European architecture altogether. These days were happily still far off even if the incipient germs of the mortal illness had already invaded the body of architecture without yet making themselves felt.[1] Bernini twisted the columns of the Baldacchino because the columns of the Constantinian tabernacle that stood over the same site had been twisted. That the original ones could not be re-used for their original purpose on account of their small scale was a matter of distress to him. So he re-erected them in front of the loggias containing the sacred relics on the four piers of the dome. He made these loggias part of the composition of the crossing; and they lead to the ultimate relic of all, the Chair of Peter preserved in the apse.

Bernini's Cathedra Petri (*50*) marks the triumphant climax of the Post-reformation Church. It lays stress upon the all important rock of Peter on which the Church is founded. The Cathedra, which enshrines the historic Chair, certainly falls into no definable category of art. It should be regarded as a spiritual symbol at the end of a long process of artistic experiences. It must be assessed emotionally in the full light of the Catholic Faith, not judged aesthetically. It could

[1] The fact that Borromini was working on the Baldacchino until 1633 is not without significance. Was its Rococo conception perhaps his? And did he have the Baldacchino in mind when he complained that Bernini usurped credit due to himself (see p. 152)?

only have been created by an implicit believer in that Faith. Bernini brought every dramatic device into play. He introduced the richest materials, a rare white-dashed black marble for the base of the altar and a brilliant red and yellow flaked jasper for the top. Bronze partly gilt is used for the figures. The effigy of the Chair appears to be miraculously suspended in the air. The four Fathers of the Church point to its scrolled legs rather than support them, for it would be an infringement of their dignity to bear upon their heads or shoulders the weight of the world's Church. Below and above the Chair clouds drift and angels soar while the Holy Spirit, brilliantly depicted in translucent glass, broods in a blaze of light and gold over the vision which is to all appearances insubstantial and divine. Nothing is clearly defined, nothing explained. The artist meant that the mystic apotheosis should appeal not to the spectator's reason but to his senses. No wonder that it provokes the violent disapproval both of the rationalist and the extreme Protestant.

In this amazing work Bernini for the first and only time departed from classical canons in practically every respect. On this account alone the new age heralded by Winckelmann could not find words strong enough to condemn it. It has never been wholly popular, and it may never be thought beautiful, even by those who cannot fail to admire its extreme virtuosity and are deeply moved by its devotional character.

There is no stronger reminder than the Cathedra Petri that Bernini was profoundly Catholic. Like Michelangelo he became more and more devout with old age, seeking earnestly to expiate the sins of a voluptuous youth by prayer and good works. He was bitterly assailed by religious scruples and experienced a short period of mysticism, when for hours on end he lay in bed contemplating a painting by himself of the Crucified One from whom an ocean of blood issued over the world. Every morning he attended Mass, communicated twice weekly, and went into retreat once a year. He regarded himself as God's and so the Church's unworthy instrument, and in his humility identified himself with the receptive mind of the ordinary religious Italian of his day. If his most Baroque work was done in youth and middle life for Urban VIII, his old age brought about a culmination of the Classical ideal in the three churches he built for Alexander VII. These were the oval S. Andrea al Quirinale, the Greek cross S. Tomàso Villanova at Castel Gandolfo and the circular Assunta at Ariccia. All are distinguished by an emphasis on horizontals and verticals and a composed approach to the age-old problem presented by the centralized formula of temple architecture. They are in other words more Vitruvian than any of his previous buildings. They reflect the influence of the Pantheon, not only in the drumless dome, ribbed and panelled within, but in the components of the interior masses. Yet they are enlivened by decorative detail, of youths holding garlands over the attic windows, and perspective altarpieces which are the hall-mark of Bernini's unmistakable style throughout his long life.

RAINALDI (1611–91) AND THE FOLLOWERS OF BERNINI

Bernini's is rightly the dominant name in the hierarchy of seventeenth-century Italian artists. The sheer force of his personality and the novel qualities as well as varied quantity of his work have made him the protagonist of the Baroque, just as Michelangelo, the giant towering over the sixteenth century, is generally recognized to be that of Mannerism. Neither claim is strictly justifiable, and it is seldom that an individual, even a Titan, is solely responsible for a new artistic movement, the outcome of many conflicting circumstances and as inevitable as the passage of time. Bernini, like Michelangelo, was always a sculptor and only a practising architect as it were by accident. His buildings were few compared with his sculpture. The contribution he made to architecture was sculptural and he invested it with a new plasticity of form it had not possessed hitherto.

Bernini's influence was immediate and far-reaching.[1] In another age some of his near contemporaries and closest followers, like

[1] An example of his immediate influence upon architecture is F. A. Picchiatti's beautiful church of Monte della Misericordia, Naples. It is obviously inspired by Bernini's S. Andrea al Quirinale. Yet both churches were begun the same year—1658.

Ercole Ferrata and Antonio Raggi, would have made great reputations for themselves. As it is their respective works owe nearly everything to Bernini; and they pale under his shadow. It was their misfortune rather than lack of talent that prevented them from emerging into full limelight. Ferrata (1610–86), who came from Como, joined Bernini's studio in his early youth. He worked for his master on the Cathedra in St. Peter's and the Scala Regia. Raggi (1624–86), who was a full generation younger than Bernini, was the most distinguished of his pupils and blessed with an almost impressionistic touch of the utmost delicacy and refinement. His figure on the Piazza Navona Fountain of Danube (*54*) leaning back from the rock with raised arms and outstretched fingers and with the toes of his right foot turned up to express tension, is a masterly summary of strength and energy. He was the sculptor of the Martyrdom of St. Cecilia in S. Agnese in Agone and of the aetherialized St. Andrew in the church dedicated to his name on the Quirinal Hill. After his master's death he was one of the few Romans to transmit a personal quality into late seicento sculpture.

Although the medium in which he worked was almost exclusively stucco, Giacomo Serpotta (1655–1732) most nearly approached Bernini's greatness as a modeller of the flesh. Serpotta, who spent nearly all his life in his native Palermo, had studied in Rome where he assimilated the Bernini spirit even though he was not the great man's pupil. The distance of Sicily in kilometres and days from Rome gave him a decided advantage over Ferrata and Raggi. He was able to develop a style entirely individual. As a stuccoist he had no rival in Europe. His little oratories in Palermo with their combination of architecture and sculpture in relief and the round—devised to frame paintings by Caravaggio or Vandyke—are the counterparts of Bernini's Cornaro Chapel in multi-coloured marbles. Serpotta went direct to life—and high life at that—for his figures which he released from conventional attitudes and even dress (*55*). His women, whether religious or allegorical subjects, are exquisite, slender creatures with wasp waists, wearing beguiling négligé, long flowing skirts and plumes in their hair. They seem to anticipate the beauties

51 *S. Girolamo della Carità, Rome: altar of the Spada Chapel (1660)*
Francesco Borromini, architect

52 *Palazzo della Consulta, Rome (1734–9)*
Ferdinando Fuga, architect

53 *Oratorio dei Filippini, Rome (1637–42)*
Francesco Borromini, architect

54   *Fountain in the Piazza Navona, Rome: the figure of Danube*
Antonio Raggi (1624–86), sculptor

55 *Oratorio del Rosario, Palermo, Sicily: figure of La Forza Giuseppe Serpotta (1655–1732), sculptor*

56 *S. Maria in Campitelli (1667), Rome*
Carlo Rainaldi, architect

of George III's reign depicted on the canvases of Sir Joshua Reynolds. And if Serpotta gave his women a patrician grace which we associate with the court rather than the convent, his children are the most natural studies in the world. Serpotta's work lies midway between High Baroque sculpture and the Rococo statuary of eighteenth-century Germany. It is less robust than delicate and at times its sentiment verges upon sweetness.

In the Kingdom of the Two Sicilies Bernini's spell evaporated slowly. Long after Serpotta's death the sepulchral chapel of the Sangro family was rebuilt in Naples. Known as the Cappella Sansevero it is lined with panels of Siena marble. The vaulted ceiling is painted in perspective. The floor is paved in powdery brown tiles. It is the most integral Baroque interior in Naples. It is incidentally a gallery of mid-eighteenth-century Neapolitan statuary. In addition to the tombs of the Sangro family a series of bow-fronted plinths against the arcades of the nave, carry statues representing Modesty, Piety, Sincerity and other virtues by Antonio Corradini, Francesco Celebrano and Francesco Queirolo, to mention the works of only three sculptors. In addition to these the famous group by the last-named artist entitled *The Disabused*, of a man disengaging himself from a net with the assistance of an angel, and the recumbent effigy of the Veiled Christ by Giuseppe Sanmartino come under the influence of Bernini. Each one of them demonstrates the arrested movement of a split second, the concentration upon a physical incident outside the actual boundaries of the group, or a technical triumph over material which were Bernini's novel contributions to sculpture. In Rome mid-eighteenth-century sculptors had long ago rejected these factors for being out of date. Instead they were returning to Hellenic repose and contemplation.

In Carlo Rainaldi Professor Wittkower[1] sees a link between Mannerism and the High Baroque. "Throughout his lifetime", he says, "Rainaldi adhered to the principle of intersecting Baroque structure with ambiguous elements." In fact Rainaldi who was born

[1] R. Wittkower, "Carlo Rainaldi and Roman Architecture of the Full Baroque", *Art Bulletin*, vol. IX, 1937.

in 1611 grew up long after the fighting days of the Council of Trent
were forgotten and flourished during the period of the Church's
new found self-confidence. He was educated by the Jesuits but had a
difference with them over a chapel they commissioned and then
cancelled. Ever after he was their bitter enemy and it is not altogether
far-fetched to see in his unorthodox elevations and plans a protest
against the hidebound Gesù concept of church architecture which
this powerful Society had enjoined upon Rome. Far from reflecting
the scattered piecemeal units of Mannerist planes Rainaldi's façades
show a wholeness and organic movement which only express the
Baroque. In their richness and concentrated purpose they have an
affinity with the pictorial façades of Martino Longhi the younger.
In their three-dimensional quality, and above all in their sense of
perspective, they derive from Bernini's influence. Yet Rainaldi was
neither a painter nor a sculptor, but an architect solely, being the
son and grandson of well-known Roman builders.

The seemingly twin churches of S. Maria in Montesanto and S. Maria
dei Miracoli in the Piazza del Popolo owe their siting and foundation
to Rainaldi, although the course of their construction was long drawn
out (57, 58). They are about the earliest, and in Rome the most celebrated, specimens of that scenographic planning which the Baroque
introduced, and register in a wonderfully beautiful manner a sortie of
three straight thoroughfares to different compasses of the City from
the northern gate. They are the sentinels to those famous vistas
which so greatly impressed Bishop Berkeley standing at the obelisk
in the middle of the piazza, as they were to impress generations of
later spectators from the same spot. Because of the divergent areas
of the two sites Rainaldi, in order to preserve a semblance of symmetry, planned S. Maria in Montesanto as an oval, and S. Maria dei
Miracoli as a circle. A subtle difference in the design of the *campanile*
of each church distracts the eye from those awkward points where the
discrepancy in width of the façades would otherwise be observable.
To both churches Rainaldi has added long choirs and to S. Maria dei
Miracoli two deep chapels at the arms.

Rainaldi's façades and plans show an originality and virtuosity

140

which were to lead to far greater liberties in eighteenth-century Germany. The façade he imposed upon S. Andrea della Valle (the church was begun to the Jesuit Padre Olivieri's design in 1589) has a serrated outline and a spatial rhythm which make a departure from

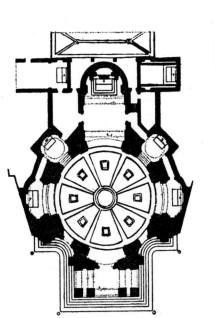 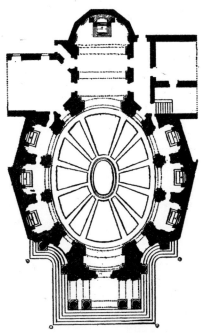

57 *S. Maria dei Miracoli, Rome*　　58 *S. Maria in Montesanto, Rome*

the old Vignolan Gesù façade. One can imagine the satisfaction with which he deliberately scrapped the designs of his Jesuit predecessor. Nevertheless the breaks of Rainaldi's front are too slight to induce those effects of depth which he was later to bring about with bolder recessions. His completion of S. Andrea precedes his rebuilding of S. Maria in Campitelli (*56*), which, begun in 1667, amplifies the characteristics of the first church.

The plan of S. Maria in Campitelli is extremely complex, being a kind of double Greek cross with a projection added at the sanctuary end. The nave proper is thus divided into three portions flanked by chapels, and narrows towards the altar. The consequence is that there is no apparent centre or axis. The hidden motifs convey the illusion of infinite space and induce infinite surprise (72). The perspective effect created by the repeated recessions is bewildering and strangely compelling. The visitor is not at first aware of the plan, so irregular does it appear to be, and excitement is added by his not knowing what he is going to find the further he penetrates the interior. There are no curves in the plan or structure, apart from the arches. The very rich effect is obtained from the free standing, fluted Corinthian columns and the projecting entablatures they carry as well as from the profusion of coloured marbles used throughout. The composition of the façade is similar to that of S. Andrea, only more complex and more deeply underlined. It is a succession of aedicules, or tabernacles. Like a Japanese puzzle-box one tabernacle fits into another, the recession of columns producing strongly delineated lights and shades. Nowhere is this motif more triumphant than in the façade of SS. Vincenzo ed Anastasio by Martino Longhi the younger, which was actually built seventeen years before the other. The S. Maria in Campitelli façade of deeply undercut planes, perpendicular and severe, emphasizes a type which became very popular in Europe. It reappeared in Rome[1] in the eighteenth century and thence spread throughout Italy, France and Germany. It is to be seen in Pompeo Picherali's remarkable front with its forward thrust which he imposed upon the Duomo at Syracuse in Sicily (59), at St. Roche and St. Eustache in Paris and St. Johann Nepomuk in Munich.

Carlo Rainaldi was only thirteen years younger than Bernini and survived him by eleven, dying in 1691. The Roman style which Bernini had in a sense created was carried into the eighteenth century by an actual pupil of a very much younger generation. This was Carlo Fontana, a great-nephew of Domenico, born in 1638. He did not come to Rome until 1650 at the age of twelve, when he is said to have been apprenticed first of all to Cortona. He worked under Rainaldi at S. Andrea della Valle and to some slight extent had a

[1] At S. Apollinare by Fuga and at S. Caterina della Ruota.

59 *Syracuse, Sicily: Duomo façade (c. 1730)*
P. Picherali and A. Palma, architects

60 *St. John Lateran, Rome: façade (1733–5)*
Alessandro Galilei, architect

hand in the design for the façade. Then with his master Bernini he helped to complete the twin churches in the Piazza del Popolo, abolishing the high attics that had been intended to crown the pediments and adding the porticos. Carlo Fontana had thus learnt his profession under three of the greatest architects of the age. He introduced a kind of picturesque elegance—traceable to Cortona— into the Roman High Baroque which was well in evidence in his imaginative church of S. Rita. Originally built under the Capitoline Hill S. Rita was swept away by Mussolini in the interests of pedantic archaeology but subsequently rebuilt close to S. Maria in Campitelli. The four fountains on the canted corners of the Quattro Fontane junction of streets are his (*30*), as is also the regal, but slightly stiff fountain in the Piazza di S. Maria in Trastevere. He had great influence upon a young Scottish pupil, James Gibbs, the future builder of St. Martin-in-the-Fields and St. Mary-le-Strand, London, in which last church the rigidity of the master's style is perceptible. But that Fontana could work in a looser, more elastic manner is evident from the façade of S. Marcello in Corso, which gives a new vigour to the Vignolan church façade of superimposed orders. Fontana lived until 1714 and was a link between Rome's High Baroque under the great seventeenth-century masters and Late Baroque of the eighteenth century, which compared with work in the contemporary style of Germany and Austria was a dwindling asset.

Alessandro Galilei and Ferdinando Fuga were born in the 1690s long after Bernini was dead. Both were Florentines who became Romans by adoption. Both were much indebted to the Bernini tradition which still feebly lingered in the City. But the style of neither is what we call full-blooded Baroque. Galilei, who left little behind him —he died aged forty-six—even spent five years in England, where he went at the beginning of George I's reign, at the instance of the British Ambassador to Tuscany, and desperately but unsuccessfully sought employment. A slight English Palladian heaviness is apparent in his work. His great façade to the Lateran Church just misses the grand opportunity offered by a superb site (*60*). In its endeavour to convey a Baroque contrast in light and shade it is a failure. The gaunt pilasters against the piers, which have no walled background, look far too flimsy to support the ponderous entablature; and the horizontal line of the balconies, although helping to reduce the narrowness of the bays, gives a disturbing impression of insecurity. Galilei was more successful with his façade of S. Giovanni de' Fiorentini.

Fuga was a greater architect. He lived to an advanced age and right into the Neo-classical period which cannot have been altogether alien to him. During the transition from the Baroque to the Rococo he managed entirely to avoid the latter style by which his contemporaries Salvi and Raguzzini were both affected. Although he lived in the eighteenth century he nevertheless belonged to the seventeenth. On first coming to Rome from Florence he learnt his art from the old Vatican architect, Antonio Valeri, who had been Bernini's pupil and was looked upon as the heir to his tradition. Fuga, whose status in the Roman hierarchy is an equivocal one, nevertheless derived from his master a benevolent propensity to the Baroque. The twenty years after 1730, when he was summoned from Florence by the Corsini Pope Clement XII, were his most fruitful. In 1750 he moved to Naples[1] where he worked for the Spanish Bourbons.

When the fourth decade of the century was dawning Rome seemed on the verge of assuming once more the lead in a new architecture. But alas, no outstanding master appeared on the scene with strength enough to lift the dead weight of her long tradition; and inspiration is a capricious and fugitive essence. Ferdinando Fuga just lacked the genius to bring about the necessary regeneration. His style was not sufficiently consistent, and when he seemed most confidently to follow a train of thought he often lost sight of it. Yet his architecture was always correct and faithful to the classical tradition in which he was brought up. He had a natural instinct for distributing his spaces, enjoyed an infallible good taste and produced a few buildings of undeniable beauty.

The Palazzo della Consultà on the Quirinal, with its nacreous tone

[1] There he built the Albergo dei Poveri and designed the façade of the Gerolomini Church with its highly polished white marble surface.

of surface and its white sculptural enrichments which Fuga began the year of his début in Rome, is certainly one of the City's handsomest palaces (*52*). Yet it is not particularly Baroque. Fuga has composed his façade from wings to centre, from crown to base in a manner opposed to the Baroque principle of expanding, centrifugal movement. Nor has he regarded it as a unit, which a true Baroque architect would have done, but has assembled three separate wall sections in isolated groups. This implies no criticism of an achievement of much loveliness. He has created a most harmonious symphony of parts. Moreover the classical purity of his central pilasters and the fine sculptural trophies over the doorway and upon the balustrade are in themselves masterpieces. An example of Fuga's strange hesitancy of style is the uncomfortable triangle formed by the rising and descending windows of the staircase within the courtyard of this palace. The distortion of the shapes of windows and pilasters is not made more acceptable by the grotesque bays on either side of the triangle.

In the oratory of S. Maria dell'Orazione e Morte, Fuga has gone straight to Bernini for his elliptical plan and coffered dome without a drum, and to Rainaldi for his façade of two stages of recessed columns and double pediment. Here he shows a real understanding of local tradition and Baroque plasticity of surface. The little church front, with its undulating surface and nervous crescendo of planes thrusting into an illimitable distance, is a picture in chiaroscuro. Finally, in the west front of S. Maria Maggiore Fuga is both derivative and novel. In adopting Galilei's theme for the Lateran Basilica he has succeeded where the other failed. This work is the ultimate affirmation of the eighteenth-century Baroque—untinged with Rococo—in sacred architecture and the most original of all Fuga's façades. He has taken the well-worn Gesù formula and transformed it into something far more exciting. With his mastery of spacing he has substituted for a giant order of flimsy pilasters two orders of detached columns to flank vertical voids. A top-heavy effect has been avoided by enclosing the voids within a triangular structure that recalls the composition of Bernini's S. Bibiana. Instead of inadequate balconies

147

cutting across the front he has imposed a firm horizontal division between the stages, and instead of a ponderous crowning entablature a delicate balustrade with correctly proportioned figures against the skyline.

61 *Palazzo di Propaganda Fide, Rome: façade by Bernini*

62 *Palazzo di Propaganda Fide,*
Rome: façade (1649–56)
by Borromini

63 *S. Alessandro, Milan (1602)*
L. Binago, architect

64 *S. Ivo alla Sapienza, Rome*
(1642–1660)
F. Borromini, architect

4. The High Baroque

BORROMINI (1599–1667)

FRANCESCO BORROMINI's influence upon architecture was to be more profound and ultimately more enduring than Bernini's. Bernini infused into the Baroque style the universal qualities of the artist; Borromini wrested from it technical achievements of hitherto unimagined daring.

This extraordinary man displayed none of the precocity or swagger of his better known contemporary. He was a slow developer and reached maturity by unspectacular stages. He was born at Bussone on Lake Lugano of a father who had been architect to the Visconti family in Milan. He began his working life in a humble capacity, and from the age of nine to fourteen was apprenticed to an engraver. That his impressionable years, which were spent in the capital of Lombardy, had important consequences in regard to his architecture will become apparent later. At the age of fifteen or so he went without his father's knowledge or consent to Rome, where he enlisted as a simple labourer under a countryman, Lione Gamo, master mason at St. Peter's. There he remained until he was thirty working as an ordinary mason. His name does not appear in the Vatican building accounts before 1624 when he is mentioned as engaged upon a new base for Michelangelo's Pietà. Carlo Maderna, then Chief Architect to the Holy See, was some sort of relation and soon recognized his unusual ability; he must have sympathized with the reserved character of the struggling mason and he did his best to help him. Borromini always remained devoted to Maderna's memory and even expressed the wish to be buried in his tomb. He assisted him on the façade of St. Peter's and at the Palazzo Barberini where

151

the earliest characteristics of the younger man's style are recognizable in several of the windows. On Maderna's death he continued to work for a time under Bernini and as late as 1633 there are records of his collaboration on the great Baldacchino over the Apostle's tomb.

But Borromini was not happy under the new Chief Architect and about this time his service with the Papacy came to an end. Clearly Bernini was as anxious for him to go as he was to leave, for in 1632 his superior advised him to accept the post of Architect to the Archinagio Romano. Nothing came of this. Whether the eventual parting was the result of an open rupture is not known, but an unpublished passage in the manuscript of Baldinucci's Life of Bernini reveals that Borromini had dared to criticize his superior. He complained that the Chief Architect's technical ability fell short of his ideals and he reproached him for arrogating to himself exclusive credit for work done by him, Borromini.

The surprising thing is that the two men could have worked together for any length of time. Their ideas and temperaments were totally opposed. Bernini was far the more traditional. His architecture was an expansion of the classical idiom to which he gave, it is true, an outward impulse boldly reaching to the stars, often in splendid disregard of detailed accuracy. Borromini's meant a contraction of space, a concentration upon the utmost refinement of pictorial effects within a narrow sphere. Bernini's art was cosmic, Borromini's cerebral and inward-looking. Chantelou records how Bernini, in speaking of Borromini's tendency to fly in the face of nature, asserted that he himself and most painters and sculptors took the human figure for the rule of proportion in their architecture ; that Borromini on the contrary based his on the forms of chimaeras. Bernini saw Borromini as a mischievous revolutionary running contrary to the accepted canons of art and good taste. His feelings are summed up in a remark aimed at Borromini : "I think it less of an evil to be a bad Catholic than a good heretic." Nothing provides a clearer contrast between their styles than the Palazzo di Propaganda Fide where the work of both men can be studied in juxtaposition (*61, 62*).

It was very important to its founders that this Palace, whence emanated the policy of the Church and where in the words of De Brosses "missionaries are fattened for the cannibals", should be dignified and spectacular. It was begun by Bernini and finished by Borromini. Of the two façades at right angles to each other one is by Bernini and the other by Borromini. Borromini therefore felt obliged —he may for all we know even have *been* obliged—to keep his façade basically the same as his predecessor's, that is to say of two storeys and an attic with vertical shafts dividing each window bay. But whereas Bernini's planes are fairly orthodox his successor's are anything but straightforward. Where Bernini was content with a simple string-course to separate attic from *piano nobile*, Borromini has a deeply projecting cornice canted at the ends and recessed in the centre. He has introduced a series of window heads of concave and convex outlines and with the weirdest crests. In other words Bernini's front, which could never be mistaken for a Renaissance design because of its novel use of vertical recessions, is none the less unexceptionally classical; Borromini's is jagged, bizarre and deliberately defiant.

Yet of the two Borromini was the more original architect, who concentrated greater thought upon his art. He may be said to have loaded every rift with ore. He was of course solely an architect. Although he began life as a mason he did not become a statuary. As a mason he brought to architecture the intimate knowledge of the practised specialist who had long handled stone. He paid loving attention to every detail of his buildings. Consequently all the elements of his buildings have a personal accent : and overloaded though his façades may at first appear to be, no detail is found to be redundant. On the contrary every detail is premeditated and plays a well defined part in the assemblage of the whole.

Whereas Bernini was always looking into space Borromini was continuously and relentlessly searching the depths of his soul. No Latin has been more introspective than he. He was solitary, celibate and deeply pious. He avoided conversation and his melancholy, nervous looks terrified strangers. Yet he was handsome, tall and well built. His clothes were always of the simplest in the dour Spanish fashion, so Passeri tells us.[1] Their only ornament was the coloured garters he wore and the rosettes upon his shoes. He spurned all honours, declined an invitation from Louis XIV to visit Paris, and rejected commissions that might have brought him renown and prosperity. He bothered little about emolument and built the Santa Casa della Madonna di Loreto (now destroyed) for nothing. Often he asked not to be paid for his work and successive Popes had to insist that he accepted money owing him. Perhaps his besetting weakness was spiritual pride for he was constantly affirming that no matter what the world had to offer he would not compromise his standards one jot to gain its favours. Consumed by a desire for perfection he was terrified lest a faulty design should diminish the tenuous essence of his ideals. "His designs", wrote Baldinucci, "were his own children", of whose welfare he was inordinately jealous. He was a strange, tragic because dissatisfied, idealist, who in an access of depression destroyed the greater number of his cherished papers and then himself.

Borromini's story has more than one point of contact with Caravaggio's. Both were rebels seeking freedom of expression and release from the tyranny of tradition. Neither believed he had attained his objective in spite of the fact that both had fervent admirers during their lifetime. Different though their natures were, at least they shared the same deeply searching mind in matters of religion, the same sharp-edged temper, the same turbulent spirit and a similar desperate end to their existence. Caravaggio is the painter of realism who wished to depict nature as it was, divorced from the conventional sentimentality with which the past had overlaid it. And was not Borromini attempting through another more abstract medium to express the same naturalism in the only way open to architecture, namely a new rhythm? He claimed that his only three teachers were —in this order—Nature, Antiquity and Michelangelo.

In following Nature as his first teacher Borromini did two things.

[1] G. B. Passeri, *Vite de' Pittori, scultori ed architetti . . . in Roma dal 1641–73.* Published 1772.

He reproduced natural objects in architectural detail in a realistic manner not hitherto envisaged; and he elaborated the curve and took liberties with the straight line according to the way he saw them utilized in nature. Architectural ornaments, which for untold centuries had been conventionalized symbols, were on his façades and in his interiors freshly culled from nature. If he carved a shell over a doorway, a lily on a fireplace, a flaming heart on a finial, tongues of flame licking a coronet on a window head, these objects became from his hands actual shells, lilies, hearts, flames and coronets, which he had observed, and no longer symbolic or heraldic objects. This naturalistic form of decoration was a novelty in classical work and had only been known in the time of the mediaeval carvers. Borromini even went further than the Gothic builders for he invested his architectural units with forms taken from nature. His astonishing twisted spire of S. Ivo alla Sapienza (*64*) resembles the horn of a Sicilian goat; the alcove arch over the entrance to S. Carlino alle Quattro Fontane is formed by a pair of wings folded tip to tip; the arch at the entry of the staircase in the Palazzo Carpegna is made of swirling smoke emitted from a pair of columns representing sacrificial altars. For a broader interpretation of Nature by means of the curve his buildings are of course renowned. Never, even with the late Romans, had buildings been raised upon such exotic plans. He was following and often advancing well beyond the Ancients. I have already suggested how the plates from Montani's book and the rooms unearthed in Hadrian's Villa may have influenced him. He elaborated the re-entrant curve of Montani's temple at Tivoli on his cupolas, duplicating the projections at S. Andrea delle Fratte. His plan for S. Ivo (*68*) may have been inspired by one of Serlio's woodcuts of a centralized church after the Antique, but Borromini turned it into the contour of a bee with folded wings in honour of Urban VIII whose crest this insect was. The plan of S. Carlino is said to derive from a room off the Piazza d'Oro in Hadrian's Villa which is a Greek cross of convex and concave curves (*25*). But the result is in effect a lemon squeezed at both ends.

Borromini was like all his generation a conscientious student of the Antique. He was careful to emphasize this claim. Whereas all his Renaissance predecessors accepted classical motifs as part of their staple material, he, like the original Greeks and early Romans, looked around him for new constituents. The Greeks invented the Doric column which they adopted from the tree trunk, perfecting its proportions, as only art dare improve upon nature, throughout the centuries. The Romans, as Vitruvius tells us, invented the Corinthian column, its foliaceous capital derived from what an architect once observed upon the roadside, namely a basket over which a flat stone had been placed and through the platted sides of which leaves of the acanthus had sprouted. Borromini in his turn, with much audacity, looked to nature to supply him with additional formulae which he then adapted to the established classical idiom. Thus he evolved the peculiar pilaster motif, called in Spain where it was to become general, the *estipite*[1], which grows slender at the base in imitation, so he postulated, of the weight-bearing human leg. The fact is his mechanical ability was such that he delighted in transposing the purposes of architectural elements. He would make a weak ornament support a load and even give the appearance of weakness to a strong member.

No wonder then that Borromini aroused severe criticism in those who regarded such novelties as contradictions of the canons of antiquity. His contemporary Baglione called his architecture "ugly and deformed" and him "a most ignorant Goth and corrupter of architecture and the infamy of our century". These are unrestrained words, and suggest personal animus in the writer. Brice[2] in 1684 complained that Borromini had reversed *ce que l'usage et la raison avaient autorisé avant lui.* Even that great experimentalist Sir John Soane, who was unique in his generation to appreciate the unconventionalities of Vanbrugh, spoke of "the excesses" of Borromini who carried invention so far as to lose sight of the simple and unaffected grandeur of ancient compositions. Soane saw little beyond

---

[1] *Estipite* meaning styptic, producing contraction. It is a sort of reversed obelisk.

[2] Germain Brice, *Une Nouvelle Description de la Ville de Paris,* 1684.

"chaotic confusion" in his work where nothing seemed clearly defined and all was without taste. And here perhaps Soane has put his finger on the Achilles heel of Borromini. The sum total of invention in any art must in its own justification amount to new beauties. Can we in all truth say that Borromini's architecture was invariably beautiful? His tortured, astringent façades are always interesting and fascinating; at times they are deeply moving. But they do not always move us to see in them the magic of a new aesthetic. And through some of his regional imitators, like for example Vaccarini of Catania, architecture assumed a weighty ugliness that is almost frightening to behold.[1]

Borromini tells us that Michelangelo was his third teacher. He certainly had an unrivalled opportunity to study the works of the great master during the years he spent at St. Peter's. And he freely adopted Michelangelesque motifs. The pilastered giant order of the Capitoline palaces is recalled by the nave of St. John Lateran: also by the lower stage of the façade and second courtyard of the Oratorio dei Filippini. Sir Anthony Blunt has pointed to certain influences upon the façade (53) of the Oratory in the portal, windows and crowning tabernacle of the Porta Pia. The serried row of scrolled crests carrying balls, which Michelangelo introduced upon that proud gateway to Rome, become constant features of Borromini's decoration. Such particular influences were inevitable; but Borromini derived from Michelangelo more than these exterior signs. In his eyes Michelangelo represented the impulse towards the perfection of the architect's ideal, rather than the perfection of architecture itself. He too became possessed by that impulse which expressed itself in tense, tight forms that were almost more Mannerist than Baroque. It is as though he sought by desperate efforts to release his tormented spirit by transfusing it into his architecture, and miscarried in the attempt.

[1] G. B. Vaccarini (1702–68), almost an exact contemporary of Bernardo Vittone, was called in 1730 to complete the reconstruction of Catania in Sicily after the devastating earthquake of 1693. He was an able master of hydraulics and mathematics, and a priest. He belongs to the tortured, celibate school.

Yet a fourth teacher, of which it did not occur to him to say anything, was surely Milan. After all he had been the devoted pupil of the Lombard, Maderna, who started his career as a Mannerist architect. They both came from the north, and Borromini never forgot the buildings he saw rising in Milan during his childhood. Whether or not he returned there in later life we do not know but there are in his buildings elements that correspond surprisingly closely to the works of the Milanese architect, F. M. Ricchini, who was his senior by sixteen years. In Ricchini's S. Giuseppe, begun in 1607 and not finished until 1630, the façade bears no relation to the octagonal plan. It belongs to the Vignolan type, but the two stages are curvilinear and agitated like those of S. Carlino and the Oratorio dei Filippini. His Palazzo di Brera and Palazzo Durini have court-yard arcades with the unusual feature of arches separated by a single lesser bay under the same entablature, forming a kind of telescoped Palladian or "Venetian" opening. This individual arrangement is found in the lower walk of the cloisters of S. Carlino. Borromini, however, develops the theme by dispensing with an additional column at each corner of the cloister, which he makes curved instead of right-angular. Several of the Palazzo Durini doorheads of varying, restless shapes, whether raised segmental curves, or segmental pediments tailing into unsupported imposts, are found reflected in Borromini's window heads at the Oratory and the Sapienza. The Palazzo di Brera was designed in 1651 and the Palazzo Durini finished in 1648. Work at these two palaces overlapped work at the Oratory and the Sapienza. It is therefore just possible that Ricchini was influenced by Borromini and not vice versa. In this case the younger had an imitator in the older, more established architect, which seems im-probable. It is surely far more likely that Borromini had access to Ricchini's designs.

There is also little doubt that Borromini was influenced by Lorenzo Binago's church of S. Alessandro, Milan, which dates from 1602. The form of this church (*63*) between two flanking towers and under a central dome finds a parallel in S. Agnese in Agone, for the plan and construction of which as far as the cornice Borromini was responsible.

65 Doorway to the Casa dei
Zuccari, Via Gregoriana, Rome
(1590)
F. Zuccari, architect

66 Entrance to the
Palazzo Doria,
Rome (1731–33)
Gabriele Valvassori,
architect

67 *S. Maria in Trastevere: Cupola of Cappella Avila (1680)*
A. Gherardi, architect

When that feature was reached he quarrelled with the heirs of Innocent X, its founder, and resigned. The remarkable undulating tympanum of S. Alessandro is not repeated in S. Agnese where movement is found instead in the concave façade. But for the tympanum of the Oratory Borromini designed a wavy skyline similar to Binago's. Finally, the window with stilted pediment within the tympanum of S. Alessandro, consisting of two arcs of a circle meeting in a point, is reflected both in those doorheads by Ricchini in the Palazzo Durini and those windowheads by Borromini at the Oratory and the Sapienza to which I have just alluded.

It was above all by rhythm that Borromini contributed to the development of seventeenth-century architecture. And rhythm is essentially Baroque. This element binds him to his own age. He was the first and greatest master of geometrical composition. To appreciate Borromini's rhythm on the site it is necessary to stand immediately under one of his buildings and look up at it. By this means you often get a better idea of its astonishing harmonies and contrapuntal movements than by observing it from the front. His façades of the Propaganda, the Oratory and S. Carlino will repay this treatment. Of the first (*11*) the great cornice in sharp projecting edges with its central inward sweep, straight flanking lines and canted angles at either extremity, like the sure flourishes of a confident draftsman's pen, is so exciting that it makes you gasp with amazement. The contrasting concave and convex windows play the same lively theme in counterpoint. The Oratory façade is still more ambitious without being so successful. The windowheads in staccato rhythm are too rapid and repetitive for us to appreciate the solemn beauty of the pilastered orders one above the other, though the rotundity of the lower centre bay and its flanking pilasters, creased down the middle like crisp paper, are most remarkable. The two stages of the S. Carlino front, however, are a fugue of contrasting themes so subtly composed that the phrase they strike reverberates in the mind long after the eyes have been satisfied.

The same daring rhythms are sounded in Borromini's interiors. When you are inside S. Ivo or Il Re Magi you are at once made aware

161

of their unconventional plans and their verticality. For Borromini draws the plan upwards from the ground to the roof. In S. Ivo the conflicting curves and sharp angles of the nave proceed through the great belt of the cornice, which seems to control the whole centralized plan, into the very ribs of the dome (it covers the entire chapel) where the outlines are repeated until they melt into the eye of the cupola. In Il Re Magi the plan is rectangular but with rounded corners. There is no dome but the slender pilasters again project the vertical lines above the cornice into the cove of the ceiling, where they dissolve into ribs in a manner which is more Gothic than Classical.

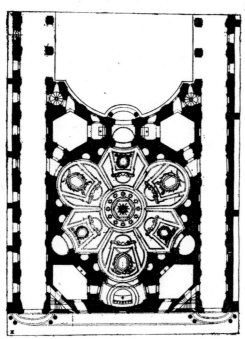

68 *S. Ivo, Rome*

On the whole Borromini is remarkably sparing of colour. Whereas Bernini was lavish in polychrome marbles, he prefers white walls and columns. Sometimes a faint light blue tint is introduced on ceilings or walls and a grey tint on floors. Only in the lovely little Spada Chapel of S. Girolamo della Carità does Borromini rely upon coloured effects (*51*). The intarsia walls inlaid with *pietre dure* in a damask pattern are hung with framed oval reliefs suspended on feigned ropes, all of marble. At the entry two alabaster winged angels holding a communion cloth take the place of rails. The wonderful drapery in deep folds is of a striped polychrome marble. The altar and floor are likewise of coloured marble intarsia. On either side of the chapel funerary effigies of the Spada family recline as at a feast of the

162

Ancients. Beside the altar are set a pair of caskets from which depend scrolls recording the virtues of the deceased.

The Spada Chapel is exceptional among Borromini's works in that it is not distinguished for architectonic effects. It is purely decorative, a work of great imagination. It is a delightful fantasy. Like the two little side chapels in S. Carlino it is a precursor of the Rococo.

FOLLOWERS OF BORROMINI IN ROME—RAGUZZINI (c. 1680–1771)

Borromini did not, like his great rival, have a school of disciples. He was not, like Bernini, regarded as the arbiter of taste, the fount of golden rules of a new architecture—at least not in his lifetime. Yet his buildings were imitated over a longer period than were those of any other Italian architect since the Renaissance. They determined the strange paths into which the Baroque was to run and finally the bog in which it foundered. His influence was not in the end to prove beneficial. It derived from the idiosyncracies of a spiritually sick man whose art was their victim as it was their expression. The phenomenon is not by any means an isolated one. History has shown in our own day how the arts have been directed into particular courses by the neuroses of individuals. Borromini was far more responsible than Bernini for the Baroque style developing into the Rococo—the Rococo which discarded the canons of Classical architecture in favour of romanticism and naturalism. The essence of these two qualities is inimical to architecture which is an abstract art, and in the end must destroy it.[1]

On Borromini's death his style went into an eclipse in Rome—for a time. Bernini, his reputation at its height, survived him for thirteen years. Then in 1680 Antonio Gherardi constructed a vault over the Cappella Avila in S. Maria in Trastevere (*67*) which for sheer poetic

[1] I have instanced the Baldacchino in St. Peter's (on which Borromini worked) as perhaps the earliest example of Rococo. As a work of naturalism in architecture the hideous Casa dei Zuccari in the Via Gregoriana, Rome (c. 1590) is a glaring example (*65*). It has a doorway in the likeness of a gaping mouth, the lintel being formed of eyes and nostril. A building of such extreme naturalism as this ceases altogether to be architecture.

fantasy hardly has an equal in Italy. Against the opening of the dome, itself formed of a balustrade in perspective, four stucco angels hover and support the base of an inner cupola. The illusion of the weight of the columned cupola resting on the slender shoulders of the winged youths is entirely in the spirit of Borromini, whose architecture is so frequently characterized by ornamental detail doing the work of functional elements. Gherardi, who was as much a painter as architect, achieved here (and again in the Cappella di S. Cecilia, in S. Carlo ai Catinari) in one medium what his contemporary Andrea Pozzo the perspective painter was doing in another.

In the following century Borromini's worst mannerisms were exaggerated by several Roman architects who kept to the letter without the least understanding the spirit of his works. Gabriele Valvassori was an imitator and his windows of the Palazzo Doria (*66*) are heavy-handed versions of the tortured and raised pediment introduced with such startling effect at the Oratory. Valvassori's heads come perilously near to a caricature of the human eyebrow and their exclamatory gesture verges on the ludicrous. Francesco de Sanctis's façade of the Trinità dei Pellegrini (1723) was the first eighteenth-century front deliberately to derive from S. Carlino. It is slightly concave in shape, but without any counterpoint, and has ogival headed niches on the lower stage. But the composition is lacking in movement and charm. Giuseppe Sardi's Maddalena façade (1735) attempts to recapture the flowing movement of S. Carlino in its concave outline and contrasting convex window over the portal and in the curved and broken pediment over the whole (*75*). But the attempt is clumsy and the hooded niches on Rococo brackets are of terrifying ugliness. The Maddalena, voluble, edgy and absurd, is the final answer to the question whether it is advisable for a talented architect to exploit the tricks of a highly eccentric genius. Sardi was far more successful in his S. Maria Zobenigo in Venice which, although very ornate, gently ascends in a crescendo of well disposed masses.[1]

---

[1] Sardi, who came from Lugano, left most of his work in Venice. He was not strictly speaking a Roman architect. He built the façade of S. Paolino alla Regola as well as the Maddalena in Rome.

There was one architect working in Rome in the eighteenth century under Borromini's influence who was far superior to any of these. Filippo Raguzzini had practised in Benevento until he was over forty. Then in 1724 he moved to Rome in the suite of Archbishop Orsini of Benevento who had been elected Pope Benedict XIII that year. During this pontificate Raguzzini enjoyed high favour but on Benedict's death only six years later fell into instant disgrace, was reviled as *architetto gotico e beneventano* and endured horrible persecution. The fact that no worse adjective than the pejorative "Gothic" was levelled at one so much resented indicates at least that his failings were hard to pinpoint. Nevertheless during his brief period of eminence, which coincided with the spread of the Rococo from France to Germany, Raguzzini almost succeeded in introducing that style to Rome. Had his august protector reigned just a little longer he might have done so. As it happened the style received no more welcome in the home of the Baroque than the Gothic, against which all true Romans have consistently inveighed. And it is probable that they even identified the one with the other as a barbaric corruption of the art which was their dearest inheritance from classical times.

Raguzzini's little church of the Madonna della Quercia is testimony of what he endeavoured to carry out. Above all he sought a strongly vertical movement by untraditional means. The orders are no longer used to suggest a structural purpose but become attenuated, decorative features applied like the strokes of a painter's brush to accentuate the palpable vivacity of his convex front. In the Church and adjoining Hospital of S. Gallicano the vertical strokes are no more structural than the curious saucer panels on the long face of the Hospital. But the effect of both is as charming as it is bold. Raguzzini's masterpiece is the Piazza S. Ignazio, a real achievement of Rococo theatrical of which the only parallel composition in Rome is Niccolò Salvi's Trevi Fountain. The houses are grouped exactly like the wings of a stage, but Raguzzini has most skilfully married them to the grave façade of the pre-existing church of S. Ignazio by keeping their pronounced cornices on a level with the base of its upper order.

The contrasting straight lines and arcs of a circle upon which the groups are planned have resulted in a piazza which is sober and vivacious, lucid and surprising and surely one of the most dramatic corners in all Rome.

GUARINI (1624–83)

Outside Rome Borromini's message was not disregarded. In the last quarter of the seventeenth century the scene of greatest architectural activity was beginning to shift from Rome. The Italian provinces, most of which had for long been looking to the Papal States to supply not only architectural inspiration but architects, were at last reviving their traditional zest for building. But even before that happened, namely in the third quarter of the century, the mantle of Borromini fell upon, or rather was practically snatched from his shoulders in his declining years, by a Theatine monk from the north, whose genius was equal to his own.

Guarino Guarini was born at Modena in 1624 and was thus a generation younger than Bernini and Borromini. He died only three years after the former, in 1683, when King Charles II was still reigning over the United Kingdom. There are few memorials of his life and up to date there has been no biography.[1] At the age of fifteen he became a novice of the recently founded Theatine Order at S. Silvestro in Rome, and received ordination in 1647. During these early years he was a student of philosophy and architecture while Borromini was at work on the interior of S. Carlino, a building which was to have much influence upon the development of his art. For a short time he lived again at Modena. Like Borromini's, Guarini's life was haunted by misfortunes, but of a sort, as far as we know, extraneous to the spiritual. At Modena the reigning Duke Alfonso was so offended by the young man's show of independence in the design of a church which he had commissioned that he obliged him to leave the city. A long, unhappy, period of exile ensued. For a while

---

[1] In 1956 an admirable little monograph, well illustrated, by Paolo Portoghesi was published in the Astra-Arengarium series, Milan.

Guarini dwelt at Parma, then at Messina in Sicily. He went to Paris and then Spain, to Portugal and even Bohemia. Circumstances made him a complete cosmopolitan. In all these different countries he built without ever once compromising his style to suit national prejudices. Even so, architecture remained a side-line with him. He was never allowed to forget that he was in the permanent service of his Order. At Messina he taught philosophy and mathematics and published a curious tragi-comedy of high moral implication, called *La Pietra Trionfante*; in Paris he taught theology and published a learned book on that subject. Finally in 1666 he was in Turin and the next year was made Engineer to the Duke of Savoy. He remained in Turin until two years before his death. At last the disconsolate exile was allowed to return to his native Duchy of Modena. But he did not remain there for long. Once again and for the last time he travelled on business to Milan where he died in 1683.

The Turin sojourn was the period of his most sustained architectural effort, and in that city the greater part of his work has survived. In other places he was singularly unfortunate. At Vicenza his most ambitious cupola was never executed; at Messina and in Lisbon earthquakes totally destroyed his churches; and in Paris and Prague later generations seeing in his works the negation of good taste demolished them to make way for inferior substitutes.

Fortunately for posterity there is Guarini's *Architettura Civile* which, although not published until 1737, had been known about ever since his death and the engravings consulted and handled. They record those of his churches that have disappeared as well as most of his buildings which survive. The *Architettura Civile* is a very different affair from previous architectural treatises in that it gives us, incidentally, the author's personal views on the science. It is refreshingly subjective, and is not merely a dull recapitulation of the rules of the Five Orders which only too often we have to comb in order to glean some vestiges of original thought. It is immensely valuable as a record of Guarini's own experiments in architecture and a brief of what he set out to achieve. It provides an intimate glimpse into the complex and fascinating mind of an important architect, such as only

Philibert de l'Orme's *Architecture*[1] (so Portoghesi points out), had hitherto vouchsafed. Architecture, Guarini is at pains to stress, is an art which, although dependent upon mathematics, seeks to gratify the senses and should not be dominated by reason. This is in some measure a restatement of the old Jesuit argument that architecture must be a vehicle with which to draw simple minds to God. But we detect an element of disingenuousness in Guarini's claim when we consider that his objective is reached by means of the most technical ratiocination that ever an architect has indulged in. Architecture, to quote him, "has the right to be as varied as possible, for it has no other end but to please the enlightened and those who have good taste and judgment". This submission that architecture has no purpose for the exoteric man lays itself open to grave objection. Once the arts restrict themselves to the initiated and become exclusive they lose their freshness and run the risk of self-extinction. In spite of Guarini's words his buildings, because of their almost miraculous beauties, still retain for the least knowledgeable lover of architecture an appeal probably transcending that of Borromini's works.

Guarini constantly refers to the duties and responsibilities of the architect—presumably, towards the client and the public as well as his own conscience. For instance, he exhorts him not to abandon the traditional building methods of the district he is working in and to pay regard to the vagaries of climate. This advice was doubtless the result of practical experience of building in northern and southern countries, in cold and hot climates. In his wide travels he invariably studied with close attention and respected the autochthonous buildings of the past.[2] He enjoins that traditional materials should always be used, but warns that even the right choice of material "does not make the fabric beautiful so much as its well-chosen disposition". The architect should not, however, in a blind adherence to traditional rules, lose sight of the intended use of his

[1] Published in nine books in 1567.

[2] *Anche i popoli più barbari dell'America*, he hazarded, *ebbero qualche sorta di case, ove ripararsi dalle ingiurie de' tempi.* "Even the most barbarous Americans have some sort of dwelling where they may shelter from the weather."

69 *Duomo, Turin: cupola of Cappella della Santa Sindone (c. 1668–1694)*
Guarino Guarini, architect

70 Cupola of the Capilla Villaviciosa
(9th century) in the Mezquita, Cordova,
Spain

71 S. Lorenzo, Turin (begun 1667): inside of dome
G. Guarini, architect

72   *S. Maria in Campitelli, Rome (begun 1667)*
Carlo Rainaldi, architect

73   *The Parocchiale, Carignano, Piedmont (1755–66)*
Count Benedetto Alfieri, architect

75   *S. Maria Maddalena, Rome: façade (1735)*
Giuseppe Sardi, architect

74   *S. Lorenzo, Turin: interior (begun 1667)*
G. Guarini, architect

fabric. "Architecture should correct the rules of the antique and invent new ones", he writes in a passage which shows a remarkable breadth of mind and a bold approach to the subject. Hitherto no one, not even Borromini, however much he may have diverged from the paths of orthodoxy, had dared openly avow the desirability of doing so at times. Guarini does not of course advocate breaking with the classical canons. Improve upon them whenever necessary is his meaning, and he gives an example—not altogether a happy one—how the Romans (in what is now the Duomo) at Syracuse altered the Greek temple to suit their own needs in a free, uninhibited spirit. Thus he means to illustrate how architecture must adapt itself to the passing years if it is to remain true to its purpose, which is to evolve new functions to meet new conditions of life.[1]

A further instance of Guarini's universality of mind is his admiration of the Gothic at a time when, as he says, "it is not at all esteemed, but rather derided, although those truly inventive men [of the Middle Ages] have erected buildings so ingenious that no one with a judicious eye can fail to recognize in spite of their lack of symmetry how marvellous and worthy of praise they are". He goes so far as to encourage sympathetic study of Gothic architecture. This positive interest is most unusual in a post-Renaissance artist. It may be due to his having seen with his own eyes the splendid cathedrals of France and Spain. It is easy enough to detect in his architecture considerable traces of Gothic (as of Hispano-Moorish) influence, especially in the vaulting of his domes which assume notwithstanding a form and rhythm absolutely original. He quickly arrived, by a process that was elaborately geometrical, at similar effects to those the Gothic builders took centuries to evolve. Guarini was an advanced mathematician and his art was intimately, or, rather inextricably, related to mathematics, perhaps even too much so. It was far removed from realism; on the contrary it tended to be abstract. In this respect he was unlike Borromini. Instead of being naturalistic his sculptural detail became formalized. For example, where Borromini would find every excuse to turn a structural

[1] Paolo Portoghesi, *Guarino Guarini*, 1956.

feature into a natural image Guarini worked in the reverse process. His herms over the entrance portals to the Cappella della Sindone, Turin, only preserve a vague semblance of human shape and become fearsome, nebulous forms that are almost surrealist. The *Architettura Civile* is primarily a geometrical treatise, from the plates of which whosoever is sufficiently trained can see how finely calculated his effects are. "Eccentric" he may have been but "irresponsible"[1] as he has been termed is an epithet not reconcilable with his scientifically-adjusted mind. For Guarini succeeded in creating in brick or stone what his predecessors and contemporaries, the Baroque ceiling-painters, Lanfranco and Pozzo, did in paint or tempera.

It is necessary to consider that when Guarini embarked in 1666—the year preceding Borromini's death—upon his decade and a half's work in Turin the Roman Baroque was a thing unknown there. The Duchy of Savoy was still very remote from the other artistic centres of Italy. Ascanio Vittozzi, who in 1584 became Court Architect in Turin, was the first Piedmontese to build in a style faintly resembling the Renaissance. He designed churches, opened boulevards and adorned squares. His Santuario di Vicoforte near Mondovì, begun in 1594 on an elliptical plan, is a magnificent conception, but the great painted dome which approximates in size to those of St. Peter's and the Pantheon was not imposed until the eighteenth century. There are indeed few pure Renaissance monuments in Turin or Piedmont dating from before the seventeenth century. The fact that Savoy territory strayed over the Alps and that the Royal house repeatedly intermarried with the Bourbons accounts for the Duchy turning to France for guidance in culture and the arts. The large Castello del Valentino, which Count Carlo di Castellamonte began in 1633 for Duchess Christina, a daughter of Henry IV, took the form of four corner pavilions, connected by galleried fronts with high roofs, in the style of the French Château de Madrid begun a hundred years before. Count Carlo's son, Amadeo, carried on this Gallic style when he transformed Vittozzi's Villa della Regina as late as 1658. In any other capital of Italy the building would by this date have been considered

[1] M. S. Briggs, *Baroque Architecture*, 1913.

foreign and hopelessly antiquated. Such was the kind of architecture which Guarini found still current.

The Court of Turin was very different from that of the Popes in Rome. It consisted of a rich aristocracy bent upon display. Its members cherished a singular desire to create detached tribunes in the churches they patronized. These tribunes were used as much for splendid receptions before Masses as for devotion. Hence they often assumed the most complicated plans and a strangely theatrical, even operatic air. Although Guarini's style was anything but French his churches in Turin adopted palatial shapes which we hardly associate with the houses of God. La Consolata, begun by him in 1679 (but decorated by Juvara in the next century and horribly overloaded at the beginning of the twentieth) resembles a palace rather than a church. It is in fact two churches in one. It consists of a series of apartments disposed as though for entertainment. You enter an elliptical hall, then take your choice of two ways up a pair of curved stairs, proceed through two domed ante-chambers lying at an oblique angle to each other, and emerge in a domed saloon before finally reaching the oval domed sanctuary. A series of delightful lesser closets is dotted around. The outside of La Consolata, built on different levels, presents a bewildering skyline of cupolas and lanterns.

This illusion of endlessly spreading side chapels, like expanding ripples after a stone has been dropped into a pond, became a distinctive Piedmontese whim in church building. The theme demanded by a frivolous aristocracy was exploited and perfected by a genius to whose mathematical mind it gave boundless opportunities for virtuosity. In S. Lorenzo, Turin, which he had begun in 1667, the year of Borromini's death, Guarini first gave full rein to geometrical experiment (74). The plan is very involved. The nave, apparently square on the outside, is all concavities within. Yet it forms a Greek cross. The entrance narthex, the sanctuary and two chapels within the transepts are separated by four altar recesses within the piers, so that in all eight equi-sized bays are formed. These are approached by convex screens in the shape of distorted Palladian openings,

175

alternately segmental and canted. The circular dome fits directly and ingeniously upon the convex screens. The concave recesses and the columns supporting the Palladian arches take away all appearance of massiveness from the fabric which seems to be upheld by the slenderest of supports. Windows, of which there are as many as six rows revealed and hidden, admit light from the drum of the dome. In addition borrowed light trickles through the crests and over the sides of the Palladian arches. The dome and cupola form of course the most novel feature of the astounding structure (*71*). All the fillings between the ribs of the vault have been suppressed. The ribs, although of stone, stand out as if they were made of gossamer. Moreover instead of meeting in a central boss they run parallel to one another, thus allowing an octagonal space in the centre for the base of the cupola—which is clearly seen up to the soffit—to rest upon.

Whence did Guarini derive this original method of vaulting? Authorities have looked to several definitive sources. The slender mediaeval ribs of the choir of Beauvais Cathedral, which he may have seen during his Paris sojourn? Or those of the ambulatory of Narbonne Cathedral, en route for Spain? Or indeed the lovely and mysterious insect-wing ribs over the ambulatory of Barcelona Cathedral in Spain itself? Because of his admiration of the Gothic these exquisite, spider-spun vaults, the finest in the world, surely did not escape his minute study. Borromini's flat, but not detached ribs on the ceilings of the Oratory and, later, of Il Re Magi, may also have given him a hint of what he could do better. Then what of the strangely vaulted narthex of the twelfth-century Duomo of nearby Casale Monferrato, where the thick ribs stand out several feet below the fillings? Here there is indeed a suspicion of Mozarabic influence, although no explanation has been advanced how it can have reached this corner of Piedmont. Guarini must certainly have known this vaulting, for in 1671 he designed a church in Casale Monferrato which was never executed. Lastly, there are the cupolas in the Mezquita at Cordova, built in the ninth century, which he could have seen during his Spanish travels (*70*). These are by far the most probable sources, for their resemblance to the dome of S. Lorenzo is too close to be fortuitous. In the Cordovan domes pairs of ribs likewise spring from eight points on the perimeter, run parallel with each other, intersect in the same pattern and leave an open octagonal star in the centre.[1]

The impression given by the interior of S. Lorenzo[2] is of lightness and infinity, those two most magical attributes of Baroque architecture. The dome over the Cappella della Santa Sindone (the Holy Shroud) is even more remarkable than that of S. Lorenzo. Here the illusion of endless distance is more pronounced (*69*). Instead of transverse ribs Guarini has formed a receding tunnel of stepped and curved arches, their ends resting on the keys of those in the row beneath. The impeccable precision of the work suggests the carefully laid twigs of a bird's nest. At the end of the tunnel the cupola appears like a glimmering star whose pointed rays issue from the Holy Ghost in a blaze of glory. The pattern is reflected in the floor of highly polished grey marble inlaid with brass stars. From the ground the multivarious sources of the crepuscular light are nowhere visible. In its descent the light is refracted and sifted by the criss-cross arches of the tunnel and the honeycomb pattern of the cove on which the airy structure rests. The kaleidoscopic method of obtaining subdued light was borrowed from Borromini's dome of S. Carlino.

Charles Emanuel II had commissioned Guarini to add the Chapel to the east end of the Cathedral, ostensibly to house the very sacred relic of the Holy Shroud but incidentally to provide a stately link between the Cathedral and the Royal Palace, which happens to be on a higher level. These needs explain to some extent the ingenious plan of three entrances, two for the public and one for the Prince and his Court. The two entrances from the Cathedral are approached up steps flanking the High Altar. Guarini obviously derived these steps from Michelangelo's stairs to the Laurenziana. Whereas S. Lorenzo

---

[1] Notably the so-called Capilla Villaviciosa. It had an immense influence upon the Mudéjar builders in Spain. For example, the vault of the Capilla de Talavera in the Old Cathedral in Salamanca, dating from 1180, has parallel ribs rising from sixteen imposts.

[2] Guarini's church for the Theatines in Paris had been constructed on a similar plan and with similar vaulting in 1665.

with its incrustations of coloured marbles, stucco and painted figures on the spandrels, corruscates with brilliance, the Cappella della Santa Sindone, lined with black, brown and grey marbles, is sad and sombre. It is no less impressive on this account. Guarini intentionally kept the sacrosanct chapel dim and mysterious. In the gloomy interior you may well suppose yourself to be the only worshipper until the murmur of praying lips gradually discloses shrouded figures kneeling in the shadows. In both buildings the virtuosity of the architecture is expressed in flights of inconceivable audacity.

If Guarini made his churches look like palaces, he made his palaces look like churches. The oval entrance vestibule to the Palazzo Carignano has a central nave and a continuous aisle behind coupled columns (76). The stairs which rise from the vestibule in two flights

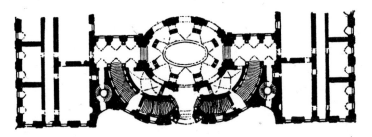

76   *Palazzo Carignano, Turin*

follow the elliptical contour while the stone treads which begin in concave shape continue after the first landing in convexities. It is impossible to over-praise the beauty of this staircase, with its smooth barreled ceiling, oval wall openings with plumelike pediments—typical specimens of Guarini's decoration—between fluted columns, and petalled balustrade. It undoubtedly had a bearing upon the development of those monumental staircases of the German palaces in the succeeding century. The serpentine façade of the Palazzo Carignano was another innovation. Guarini must have modelled it on Bernini's first tentative design for the Louvre, to which he probably had access while in Paris during the master's visit in the summer of 1665. Whereas Bernini's elevation was of a giant order set on a plinth of steps, Guarini's is set on a high base which comprises entry and mezzanine floor. His base is less successful than Bernini's plinth because it is too high. But the unusual plan of central convexity flanked by concave wings and end pavilions of four bays is the very same. So too is the recessed drum-like attic storey over the central convexity. This beautiful and compelling front (its date is 1680) is the first to have been built for a palace in an undulating contour and in brick. That designs for palaces and churches in Piedmont were almost interchangeable is borne out by Benedetto Alfieri's Parocchiale at Carignano, finished eighty years later but still thoroughly Baroque (73). For this rose brick church was obviously inspired by the Palazzo Carignano in Turin with a difference. Instead of a protuberant it has a hollow centre.[1] If you did not know before-hand you would naturally suppose it was a palace and not a church. The plan of the interior is most unusual, being that of a fan. The entrance narthex is formed of a semi-circle of Corinthian columns under a semi-dome. The sweep of the nave has a barrel vault and the circumference wall is adorned with Corinthian columns where the ends of the fan ribs would be. Unconventional though the plan is, it is also practical, for the high altar can be seen from every point. Alfieri's church resembles some gorgeous structure put up for a *fête-champêtre*. It is not altogether unlike the ephemeral banqueting-room Robert Adam erected for Lord Derby's party held at the Oaks one summer evening in 1774.

JUVARA (1678–1736)

Guarini is recognizably the direct offspring of Borromini—to use a somewhat paradoxical term in assigning fatherhood to the most solitary and celibate of Roman architects. He belongs to that family of Baroque architects who trace their descent from the no less celibate Michelangelo. The composition of their works is reflective of inward spiritual and emotional torment; and the ultimate

[1] The Church of the Crociferi in Milan, begun in 1708 by C. F. Pietrasanta has a convex front of brick, clearly under the influence of Guarini.

expression is primarily cerebral and only incidentally aesthetic. Guarini happened through circumstance to settle for a time in Turin, where he was able in fifteen years to produce a crop of buildings of such marked individuality that they determined the style of Piedmontese architecture for a century. Yet he was always regarded as a foreigner in Piedmont. The next notable figure on the Piedmontese stage was also a foreigner and cosmopolitan, who like his predecessor built in several countries of Europe outside Italy. Unlike Guarini whose following was confined to Piedmont, his influence upon European Baroque was widespread.

Filippo Juvara was a Sicilian, born at Messina in 1678 of a family of silversmiths. He was early destined for the Church and became a secular priest, although his duties in this office appear to have been nominal. At any rate he remained a celibate, but it is important to emphasize that neither his character nor his art expresses the harassed mind of the introvert. His portrait shows a face of straightforward intelligence confronting the world with assurance. He went as a young man to Rome where he studied architecture under Carlo Fontana, and in 1706 was elected a member of the Academy of St. Luke. He was introduced to the Papal Court where he seems to have been principally occupied with theatrical designs. He was taken into the service of Cardinal Pietro Ottoboni who was generally acknowledged to be the most discerning patron of artists and musicians since Queen Christina's death. Still, he travelled much, and by 1714 was Architect to Victor Amadeus of Savoy, then King of Sicily and later of Sardinia. He was employed by the King in the capacity of plenipotentiary (just as Rubens a hundred years before was invested with the same duties by his sovereign, Isabella of the Netherlands) and under the cloak of an artist was able to fulfil various useful missions. He went to Lisbon, where he may have suggested some preliminary designs for the colossal Palace of Mafra; possibly to London and Paris; to Rome again, where he projected a sacristy at St. Peter's for Clement XII; and finally to Spain, where he made plans for the country palaces of La Granja and Aranjuez and, while embarking upon the Royal Palace in Madrid, died there of influenza in 1736.

It was, however, in Piedmont in the service of the house of Savoy that Juvara concentrated his chief work and there it is still to be found. There the shade of Guarini hovered over him and the spirit of that convoluted genius breathed upon him—but not with hurricane force.[1] Juvara was always a slightly recalcitrant medium. Celibate though he too was, his architecture has a far more genial bearing than that of either Guarini or Borromini. Of the latter's work in Rome he became a passionate admirer, for by the beginning of the eighteenth century the rising generation were modelling themselves upon him rather than his great rival, Bernini. Yet Juvara was the pupil of Fontana (as we may see from the façade of S. Christina, Turin, modelled on his master's façade of S. Marcello, Rome) and from this disciple of Bernini he learned the rudiments of the architectural science. The Antique, the theatre, the Borrominiesque geometry, the apprenticeship to Fontana and, finally, the new French style of decoration are, in this order, the outstanding influences upon this important architect.

In the great convent church of the Superga (*1*)—that proud and splendid corruption of *super terga montium*[2]—built on a dominant peak outside Turin to celebrate our Lady's blessed intervention when the French were besieging the city in 1706, Juvara's design is somewhere less than halfway from the Roman Pantheon to S. Agnese in Agone. The great rotunda with its projecting portico is, like Hadrian's prototype, stiff and staid. The spherical dome, the coupled columns projecting from the drum, and even the twin *campanili*, thrust back instead of forward, are adaptations of those corresponding features of S. Agnese, it is true, but their Baroque quality is less pronounced than the classical demeanour of the whole. The incomplete façade of the Palazzo Madama, begun for the widowed mother of the King, has little that strikes us as Baroque. It too is

---

[1] Oddly enough Juvara's most Guariniesque architecture was to be found in Messina (before the earthquake of 1908). As a boy he was much influenced by Antonino Maffei, a great friend of his family. Maffei, who adopted many of Guarini's decorative tricks, was the original and perhaps the strongest link between the two architects.

[2] Meaning literally: "Upon the flanks of the mountains."

tight and staid. Composed of vertical lines it has not a curve of any sort. There is in it more than a hint of Bernini's final design for the Louvre front to face the Tuileries and a striking similarity to the central garden block of Versailles, which the French widow of Charles Emanuel II upheld as the hall-mark of sovereignty. Juvara was at the very end of his life to repeat this Bernini-Versailles composition in the Royal Palace of Madrid for Philip V of Spain, the grandson of the Roi Soleil.

The interior of the Palazzo Madama is however quite a different affair, which its French academic façade absolutely belies. With the great staircase in two flights, that comprise all but two bays of the whole "Juvara" front of the palace, we come to something essentially Italian and of its epoch. In reality the staircase-well occupies a long, narrow vaulted tunnel, with nothing of a tunnel's gloom about it (77). It is lit, not only by the high windows of the *piano nobile* but by the upper mezzanine windows as well. Juvara invoked his deeply tutored sense of dramatic perspective. He based the approach on a low columned hall whence on either side he made straight flights ascend, as it might be from the basement hall of an English Palladian house, such as Nostell Priory. Only on reaching the first landing and turning round are we confronted by the stupendous vista of window, wall and ceiling. This staircase is extremely grand in the Roman tradition and yet not at all straightforward. The pairs of columns supporting the vault of the lower hall are imprisoned in the walls in the manner Michelangelo first introduced in the Laurenziana. Moreover a kind of running-together of structural detail is noteworthy. For example, the keystones of the arched doorways of the lower hall are twisted so as to become consoles supporting the stair balustrade overhead. This is very economical and ingenious and gives a liquidity to architecture which is unsurpassed.

Juvara's architecture was certainly not always of the Berniniesque-Classical variety. The interior of his Church of the Carmine has side-chapels each lit from above by two domes, one over the altar, the other over an upper gallery with a rail round the eye, in a manner frequently practised by Fischer von Erlach before him. The chapels

182

are screened from the nave by those strange perforated arches with plumed and scrolled crests, some bearing escutcheons, of which Guarini was so fond. The brick campanile to this church, with its serpentine sides, is inspired by the drum of Borromini's S. Andrea delle Fratte.

The plan of the Palazzo Stupinigi (*80*) outside Turin is intricately geometrical and spreads over an enormous area. Seen from the ironwork *clairvoyée* the impressive forecourt is formed of separate blocks of dependencies joined to the central rotunda at obtuse angles. The result is that when inside the palace one is extremely confused. But this confusion gives way to a succession of rare delights. Never has a palace comprised such a series of marvellous apartments of varying shapes and quantity of painted decoration. The rooms are all subordinate to the central saloon, which is a stage setting turned to architecture (*78*). Indeed it can even be related to one of Juvara's scenographical designs for the Turin theatre. It is aisled and galleried, emphasis being upon verticality and a staccato curvature of outline. Dome, vaults, walls and piers are painted by the brothers Valeriani with emblems of the chase (which are even introduced upon the ormolu candle sconces), for the Stupinigi was begun as a modest hunting box. The original chandelier and furnishings make this saloon one of the most magnificent and beautiful in Europe. The decoration is in a sense reflective of some of the later Versailles apartments, but without any of the Rococo motifs which were introduced to Louis XIV's court after 1700. It is as though Juvara had in mind here the decoration carried out under Colbert's severely academic eye by J. H. Mansart and Lebrun, to which he has given a rhythm definitely Baroque. He is the first Italian architect to look to France even for a grain of inspiration.

Juvara was, then, an eclectic. Unlike Guarini, whose work was distinctive and unvarying, Juvara was variable. His buildings assumed different qualities in different countries. He never settled in any place for long and was constantly on the move. Yet in a Rococo age he remained Baroque. His architectural members were always correctly traditional, however much his robust cornices and isolated columns were calculated to obtain the best effects of chiaroscuro and plasticity. His decoration was free from broken, disruptive motifs. Juvara was immensely prolific. Ideas flowed from him in torrents, as his swift and often impressionistic sketches testify. Finally, he put more into his art than mathematics. All his buildings, as well as being interesting, are extremely beautiful.

VANVITELLI (1700–73)

Of Juvara's disciples Luigi Vanvitelli was the most important. He more than any other Italian architect determined the final phase of the Baroque style. In all his work his master's influence is discernible. He inherited from him that Vitruvian strain with its slightly French academic flavour which in the end was to merge the Baroque in a respectable Neo-classicism. He eschewed Guariniesque fantasy. He fairly refined the High Baroque from decorative irrelevancies. His buildings are the very reverse of Rococo, being purely architectonic, reasoned yet impulsive, grand yet dramatic, masculine yet passionate.

Vanvitelli was that rare thing, an artist Neapolitan born. Even so he cannot claim to be of Neapolitan breed for his father Gaspar, a distinguished landscape painter, was an Italianized Dutchman whose surname had been Van Wittel. The son went to Rome for his training and studied under both Carlo Fontana and Juvara. In Rome he measured the remains of antiquity and immersed himself in the treatises of the *cinquecento* architects, particularly Vignola. From these sources he imbibed a spirit of austerity and reserve which brought him into greater sympathy with the art of the Renaissance than that of his own time. He is said to have followed with attention the success of Palladianism in England and to have admired the sober academism which had distinguished French architecture under Louis XIV.

In 1732 Vanvitelli at S. Domenico, Urbino, built the first Neopalladian interior, thus anticipating the Classical revival initiated later in the reign of Pope Clement XII. Under that Pontiff he became Architect to St. Peter's. Although Vanvitelli did a certain amount of

77 *Palazzo Madama, Turin: the Staircase (1718)*
Filippo Juvara, architect

78   *Palazzo Stupinigi, Turin: the Great Saloon (1729–31)*
Filippo Juvara, architect

work in Rome it is in the Kingdom of Naples that his most important architecture is found. Pre-eminent as regards size and the nobility of certain features is, of course, the Palace of Caserta, begun for Charles III in 1752 and continued for his son, Ferdinand I, until 1774.

The enormous building is in plan a rectangle which encloses four large courtyards. Vanvitelli took from Juvara's design of the Royal Palace of Madrid not only the end and central tetrastyle projections but the setting upon a deep basement. The two extremely long fronts are admittedly monotonous. The serried windows and the detailed ornament are lost in the enormous bulk like a small necklace upon the bosom of an immoderately fat woman. The eye tires from following the vertical pilasters in that way it does in watching from a railway train the telegraph poles slip by ceaselessly one by one. Vanvitelli intended a central cupola and four corner towers; lack of funds did not allow his son, Carlo, to provide this relief when after the father's death, work reached the roof.

It is easy enough to level a charge of monotony against a building of these proportions. Caserta is nevertheless a noble monument. Were its elevations positively distasteful the palace would still be redeemed by the stupendous central staircase which is one of the Baroque masterpieces of eighteenth-century Europe. It is set in the very middle of the composition where the inner arms of the four courtyards meet in a cross. The staircase has frequently been described in detail. In its perspective lower hall, through which are seen an incomparable vista of the park and cascade at one end, and the long wide avenue of plane trees striding in the direction of Naples at the other, and in its upper hall with ring of piers clustered in wedge formation and supporting a saucer dome with spiral coffering, the immense composition is like some Bibiena scene transformed to stone and marble. And what a choice of stones and marbles! Only a very great artist could have conjured up such an irradiation of subtle greys and pinks. Nothing is outrageous here in colour or design. Each shade, like each unit, marries sublimely with its neighbour. The transitions are as measured and gradual as the ascents of each stair flight. The Halberdiers' Hall and the Guards' Hall are among the most beautiful apartments in all Italy, and so Gallic in style as hardly to qualify as Baroque art; the Chapel is copied unashamedly from that at Versailles.

Vanvitelli's church of SS. Annunciata in Naples, begun in 1760 and finished by his son, Carlo, is not by any means Gallic. It is Roman and it may be compared to Rainaldi's S. Maria in Campitelli because of its imaginative Baroque plan. The wide nave is preceded by a vestibule. The shallow transept is duplicated behind the altar rails within the sanctuary. Vanvitelli has made great play with his pairs of fluted marble columns. They pinpoint the perplexing contours of the church so emphatically that the eye is obliged almost involuntarily to trace out the plan. Like a clever forester who induces a person on entering a small wood to believe that endless rides have been cut into the distance, the architect has tried to mystify by suggesting vistas which do not in fact exist. SS. Annunciata is distinguished by the superb quality and restraint of its detail, of which only the heads of doors and the cupola windows are unclassical. The decoration is very successful. The coffered ceiling is treated in grey and white: the walls in grey and green. Vanvitelli was a master of subdued tones. In fact he was an artist of unexceptionable taste.

VITTONE (1705–70)

The curious thing about Piedmontese architecture is that it practically skipped the Renaissance and plunged headlong into the Baroque, which remained its element for over a hundred years. After Guarini's death it seemed to settle into a more ordered and composed condition under Juvara and his contemporaries, of whom Francesco Gallo, creator of the superb dome at Vicoforte and numerous brick-built churches, was an architect of great distinction. But this state of comparative calm did not endure for long. About the time of Juvara's death Guarini's spirit rose again with a vengeance in the person of Bernardo Vittone, the strangest individual of them all.

Vittone was born a Piedmontese in 1705 and duly went to study

188

architecture in Rome. In 1732 he won the Corso Clementino prize at St. Luke's Academy which Juvara had carried off twenty-six years previously. The following year he returned to Turin with a letter of recommendation to the Court from the well-known art patron, Cardinal Albani. He appears to have settled in Turin for the rest of his days. Little is known of his life beyond the facts that he was a queer, quirky bachelor, rich but extremely mean, and utterly absorbed in his art. More important is the evidence of his deeply religious and even mystical nature. He built numerous churches, none of large dimensions, in Turin and the surrounding district. In 1760 he published *Istruzioni elementari* ... which included a confusing treatise upon the relation to architecture of the intervals in musical composition. These he claimed—and he was not the first to do so—an architect must master if he hoped to arrive at good proportions in his buildings.

Vittone likewise belongs to the celibate, geometrically-minded school of tormented, introspective architects which I have traced through Guarini and Borromini back to Michelangelo. The similarities of character in this succession of androgynous geniuses have stamped Italian Baroque architecture with a consistently pious melancholy which is lacking in the Germanic countries where even churches appear gay and secular. Of all these architects' works Vittone's were surely the most extraordinary. Brinckmann[1] speaks of his style as the Italian Rococo. But it is less Rococo than Borromini's in that his designs show less tendency to romanticism and his architectural detail is no more naturalistic. The interiors of Vittone's churches remain, for all their unexpectedness, architectural rather than decorative. What ornament they display is unremarkable and its quality is generally poor.

The eccentricity of Vittone's architecture is not apparent in his exteriors. His skylines often consist of a dome smothered by small square towers with ogival roofs, as at S. Bernardino at Chieri (1740–44). His façades are orthodox enough, or at least what we have come to look upon as usual throughout the previous hundred years. Pilastered

[1] A. E. Brinckmann, *Theatrum Novum Pedemontii*, 1931.

projections, vertical and almost Gothic, make S. Francesco, Turin
(1761), for example, look like an elevation by Hawksmoor—so long
as we disregard the windows (82). These invariably assume those
conventionalized shapes first introduced by Guarini, either kidney,
fan, half-moon, the flaming heart or bull's eye, the last with the ogival
or drooping pediment that melts incongruously into the surround.
But Vittone's interiors are another matter. He follows Borromini in
the subtlety of his involved plans, Guarini in the pattern of his units
and Bernini in his concealed lighting effects.

His favourite plan was a basic Greek cross, usually of six to eight
bays in all, inscribed within a circle or ellipse and a long, often
rectangular sanctuary added. The nave of S. Bernardino, Chieri, is a
Greek cross, composed of four arcs of a circle united by convex angles.
The weight of the circular dome is entirely taken by the four arches
of the crossing. Beyond the arc of the altar bay an oval sanctuary
has been added with an oval dome supported by pendentives over
four piers. Both domes are pierced with concealed openings for light
and the spandrels of the nave dome have artificial rays darting
through spade-shaped cavities. The plan of S. Maria della Piazza
(1751) in Turin is an ellipse with six arc-shaped chapels attached. A
central shallow, elliptical dome is set transversely over the nave and
contains eight half-moon windows between thick ribs (49). The flat of
the dome is painted. Vittone elaborated his domes by means of the
most fanciful structural devices. That over the square sanctuary of
S. Maria (for again there are two domes to this small church) has at
each corner a motif peculiar to Vittone—what Professor Wittkower
has called an "inverted squinch".[1] Where you expect the dome to
rest upon the four spandrels over the piers you find, not convex
projections to give additional support, but concave recessions. These
are filled with windows in a manner which is disturbing rather than
reassuring. Such bravado of engineering is as it were a defiance of the
laws of construction, for just where the eye demands solidity it is
deprived of it. Vittone does not disclose why and where he came upon

---

[1] A squinch in the words of the *Oxford Dictionary* is: "A straight or arched
support constructed across an angle to carry some superstructure."

this extraordinary device, but he may have found a precedent in the octagonal lantern over the crossing of the Romanesque Duomo at Casale Monferrato where the angles are hollowed out.

Another way of treating his domes was to provide false inner domes. In the little sanctuary church at Vallinotto (1738–39), his earliest building (*81*)—of serpentine plan—Vittone has followed Guarini by making his lowest dome of criss-cross ribs without fillings. Between the ribs which are painted with flowers and cherubs you look into a second dome painted with flying angels. In the middle of this second dome is a large hole through which a third, the real outer dome, also painted, is seen. Beyond it the crowning lantern is visible. This humble wayside chapel, with its peasant-style decoration, is in fact of a most involved and sophisticated construction. The dome vista, albeit on a minute scale is actually a bolder version of François Mansart's Invalides dome in Paris or that which he designed for the Bourbon Mausoleum at St. Denis. Vittone is not known ever to have visited Paris, or even France, but he claimed to be the disciple of Juvara who was manifestly affected by the architecture of Louis XIV's reign.

On the other hand, in devising this particular dome vista at Vallinotto, Vittone was probably mindful of a more immediate precedent. Ferdinando Bibiena, the best known member of a family of eight theatrical scene artists, had built and decorated a most unusual church in Parma. This is the Church of S. Antonio Abate. True, it has no dome; but Ferdinando provided the whole nave with a false inner ceiling. Made in the mere thickness of one-inch boards, the inner ceiling is perforated with numerous openings in diverse Rococo shapes, through which the real nave roof is revealed some six foot or so above. Upon the white plaster surface of the outer roof are painted vignettes of scenes pertaining to S. Antonio Abate. These vignettes when viewed from the entrance to the church appear to fit into the frames upon the lower ceiling. The effect is very striking at first sight. But as you walk up the nave the scenes necessarily shift from their frames and a strange and rather ludicrous confusion results. Nothing more theatrical or unconventional can be imagined than the composition of the nave roof of this church. Vittone must almost certainly have seen it.

It is, however, Guarini's influence which predominates throughout Vittone's art. Now Vittone published the posthumous *Architettura Civile* in 1737, even adding some plates of his own designs. Over and over again he reproduces Guarini's geometrical features. In addition to the multivarious shapes of windows, which I have already specified, he favoured screen-like arches, their coxcomb crests pierced with bulls' eyes, to separate side chapels from nave. When Vittone was employed to redecorate the Lombardic Cathedral at Asti he even painted within a Gothic bay such a screen with a feigned sky above it. His actual chapels were often lit from concealed windows in domes and slits in spandrels. The capitals to his columns are more naturalistic and his cartouches and finials assume more vegetable forms than Guarini's; his detail approximates to Borromini's. He has a fondness for delicate ironwork railings to his galleries which run in and out of his naves like Puck's girdle, keeping the aery composition together and giving an emphasis to the plan. His plans are more rewarding even than Guarini's. In his more ambitious churches, such as the Assunta at Riva, near Chieri (1766–67) which is merely a moderate-sized parish church, he introduces four domes. Three, including the largest which covers the whole nave, are octagonal. The result—for this interior is exceptionally delicately painted—is an unearthly creation of ineffable beauty. Domes elliptical, spherical, octagonal, and semi-domes spring from his churches like a cluster of toy balloons from a single string, and such is his mastery of the science of construction that of all the Baroque artists so far considered he most nearly achieves the impossible in architecture, which is to induce the beholder to suppose that his buildings are sustained by supernatural means.

POZZO (1642–1709)

Andrea Pozzo is better known as the painter of colossal ceiling perspectives than as an architect. He happened to practise both painting and architecture and each art was so governed by the other that one can find no artist whose painting was more architectural nor whose architecture was more pictorial. Pozzo belonged to a generation midway between that of Guarini and Juvara—he was born in 1642—and although his rôle in the High Baroque scene is a unique one, he too must be classified as a member of the celibate, introspective school. Though Pozzo's greatest work is in Rome where he lived for over twenty years, he was not a Roman even by adoption; he was a cosmopolitan who exerted greater influence upon Austrian and German Baroque art than Italian.

Pozzo came from Trento in the Alto Adige, for which reason the Germans have tried to claim him as one of themselves. He was of course thoroughly Italian by birth and training, having studied in Milan, where in 1665 he became a lay brother of the Society of Jesus. He was never a priest in spite of his frequently being referred to as Padre Pozzo. All his life was spent subject to Jesuit discipline and in Jesuit service. His self-portrait in the Uffizi Gallery shows a deeply serious young face with an air not so much of spiritual as of artistic concentration. Appropriately enough he has depicted himself high up under the vault of some church pointing to his own handiwork. Pozzo's painting, like that of the vast majority of his contemporaries, was profoundly religious and, although the Jesuits must have regarded him as their approved instrument, he most likely regarded them as the medium that best suited the practice of his art in God's service. Indeed for such a one, by nature dedicated and without worldly ambition or desire for gain, no other vocation offered the same freedom from actual want, responsibility or care.

Pozzo's first painting on a monumental scale was the Apotheosis of St. Francis Saverio on the nave vault of the Jesuit church of that saint's name at Mondovì in Piedmont. Here in 1679 he produced a perspective architectural fantasy,[1] seemingly more secular than

[1] The only parallel to Pozzo's fantasy in Italian art is found in the *guglie* of Naples. These pyramids or obelisks of stone and marble rise in a crescendo of statues, medallions, half moons, clouds and drapery to the glory of our Blessed Lady and the Saints. They are a sort of Baroque apostrophe of worship, an exclamation of religious fervour. They were much favoured by the Jesuits and assumed even more fantastic shapes and decoration in Austria.

spiritual, in a colonnade of projecting columns supported on curious double trusses and a central balcony with figures. The architecture is very precisely considered and already we have those brilliantly glowing colours which we associate with Tiepolo's brush. But the work for which he will always best be remembered is the nave ceiling of S. Ignazio, Rome (79), begun in 1688. It is the logical conclusion of that earlier Jesuit decoration which Gaulli (Baciccia) had finished on the Gesù vault five years before. The two Roman churches indicate the zenith of the Society's power and the acme of that theatrical decoration with which its members invested the houses of God.

The Church of S. Ignazio was a concentrated masterpiece of Jesuit art. It had been begun in the pontificate of the Jesuit-loving Gregory XV, under the patronage of the Ludovisi family, by Orazio Grassi, a Jesuit Professor of Mathematics who had exchanged opinions with Galileo. On Grassi's retirement Padre P. A. Sasso, also a Jesuit, completed the building. The area covered by Pozzo was enormous. It included the whole of the nave ceiling above the cornice. To all intents and purposes he created with his brush in fresco a second huge church over the actual one. Gone is the stucco picture frame and gone are the stucco figures with which Raggi and others had enclosed Gaulli's ceiling of the Gesù nave and adorned the clerestory windows. In S. Ignazio Pozzo has included the clerestory windows in his composition, making the spandrels between them the base of his gigantic feigned structure. On this base he has contrived a continuous colonnade supported by columns which break the entablature in an advanced Baroque manner. At the foot of the colonnade he has painted groups representing the four continents to which the Society had brought the Gospel. In the open sky above, St. Ignatius Loyola is being received into Paradise. Pozzo never excelled this work wherein he strove to express the infinite, which was the seventeenth-century Church's invariable answer to that pagan finitude re-affirmed by the Renaissance in buildings with closed vaulting. And the effect the ceiling has upon the visitor who gazes at the ethereal vision is truly one of rising from the ground as it were in a momentary, mystical levitation. Pozzo's ceiling in the Marmorsaal

79 *S. Ignazio, Rome: detail of the Entry of St. Ignatius into Paradise; ceiling fresco by Andrea Pozzo (begun 1688)*

80 *Palazzo Stupinigi, Turin (1729–31)*
Filippo Juvara, architect

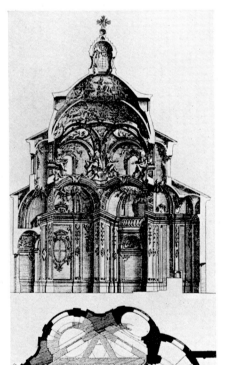

81 *(left) Santuario del Vallinotto,*
Piedmont (1738–9)
Bernardo Vittone, architect

82 *S. Francisco, Turin (1761)*
Bernardo Vittone, architect

of the Liechtenstein Garden Palace, Vienna, for all its ingenuity and feigned "inverted squinches"—as it were in anticipation of the Vittone conceit—is far less impressive on account of its comparative lowness and the obtrusive awkwardness of its cove.

The S. Ignazio ceiling was the first fresco of architectural perspective over a very large area to give the illusion that the ceiling and walls of a church were open to the sky. Throughout Italy and the continent it had its imitators. The brothers Francesco and Giuseppe Melani's Apotheosis of St. Matthew at Pisa was a deliberate copy down to the treatment of the architectural detail. In Bavaria and Austria the schools of Cosmas Damian Asam and Martino Altomonte derived their inspiration from it.

Pozzo never had the opportunities to indulge his actual architecture on the same lavish scale as that of his counterfeit architecture, but the style of the first can be detected in the second in a rather tempered form. For instance he invented a column which bent outwards at the base, called it a "sitting column" but never as far as is known put it into practice. In all his designs he endeavoured, as he tells us in his book on perspective, "wonderfully to deceive the eye".[1] Milizia, who naturally detested the Baroque because he was the firm advocate of Raphael Mengs's Neo-classicism, dismissed him in the phrase: "Whoever wishes to become an architect of what is wrong-headed, should study the architecture of Fra Pozzo"[2]—thus implying of course that Pozzo was a follower of Borromini. His projected designs were very much more bizarre than his executed works, which were restrained by his natural good taste. These have a polychrome quality deriving from the deep Venetian tones of his paintings—a quality which Borromini's works lack. His Chapel of St. Ignatius Loyola in the Gesù on which he worked from 1696–1700 surpasses in richness of material and inlay any comparable work outside Naples. The design, which is straightforward enough,

[1] Pozzo's *Rules and Examples of Perspective*, published in Rome in 1693, was translated by John James of Greenwich and dedicated to Queen Anne in 1707.

[2] Francesco Milizia, *Le Vite de' più celebri architetti*, 1768.

consists of a tabernacle of concave contour with broken entablature. The great structure is flanked by marble groups. The four columns of the tabernacle are inlaid with lapis-lazuli and gilt bronze. The architrave is of verde antique. On the cornice, angels support a globe of the world said to be the largest solid piece of lapis in existence. The name of Jesus is inscribed upon it in crystal.

The embellishment of the chapel aroused the keenest curiosity and interest in the citizens of Rome. While votes were being cast to choose the sculptor of the Saint's figure, a crowd gathered impatiently in the street to await the issue. The choice fell upon the Frenchman, Pierre Legros, who executed the figure in laminated silver. Legros also carved the group of the virgin, Religion, overthrowing the hag, Heresy, in marble. The victim is lying upon and crushing in her fall an enormous tome entitled "Martin Luther", while an angel quietly tears the pages out of another unspecified, but doubtless heretical, volume.

5. Conclusion

I HAVE tried to demonstrate that the Baroque was essentially a religious manifestation, Catholic and primarily Roman. How wilfully the Victorians associated it with heathenism and how gleefully they deemed it antichrist! To J. A. Symonds it was representative of the profane culture which he professed to believe the Counter-reformation wilfully disseminated. In identifying the Baroque with the Bolognese school of painting he wrote: "Very little of it bears examination now. We regard it with listlessness or loathing. We turn from it without regret. We cannot, or do not wish to keep it in our memory."[1] In that Baroque empiricism was the very antithesis of Church of England pragmatism: Symonds and the nineteenth-century Whig writers gave vent to sentiments more understandable than rational.

The Catholic and Roman origin of the Baroque accounts then for the preponderance of ecclesiastical and Roman buildings described in the preceding pages. Had this book been entitled *Italian Seventeenth and Eighteenth-Century Architecture,* less emphasis might have been given to the churches of the Holy City. References would have been distributed rather more evenly over other regions of Italy, equally rich in lay and ecclesiastical works of these centuries. As it is, nearly everything most original in the Baroque style of architecture emanates from Roman sources. The next important influences upon the style's development derive from Piedmont. And so, after introducing the colossal personalities of Bernini, Borromini and their disciples, I have concentrated upon the names of Guarini, Juvara and their followers.

[1] J. A. Symonds, *The Catholic Reaction,* 1886.

I have purposely laid stress upon those artists who directed the Baroque movement, to the neglect possibly of many eminent men who pursued it. Consequently the names of some well-known Italian architects have been omitted and those of others barely touched upon. For this I do not offer apologies in a book that makes no claim whatever to be comprehensive and merely skims the surface of a particular phase of art.[1] Objections may be raised that Venetian Baroque has been totally overlooked and Neapolitan Baroque too summarily dealt with. In regard to the first charge I do not underestimate the grand achievements of Baldassare Longhena (1598–1682). Although his career coincided exactly with that of Bernini, Longhena's buildings, with the single exception of S. Maria della Salute (see page 111), are little affected by the style of his great Roman contemporary. On the contrary Longhena, a Venetian by birth and throughout his life, was nurtured in the enduring tradition of Sansovino. He actually began his career as a sculptor under Sansovino's follower, the Palladian Scamozzi. Of a placid and determined temperament, Longhena brought about no dramatic revolution in Venetian architecture. Step by step he perfected in Venice a method of building which caused no more marked break in style than that made by men of the early Renaissance in following upon the heels of those of the quattrocento Gothic. His Palazzo Pesaro and Palazzo Rezzonico on the Grand Canal, massive and rusticated as they are, only depart from mediaeval defensiveness in their greater amplitude, which speaks of Baroque wealth and confidence. Both palaces owe much in their richly sculptured and arcaded top storeys to the Old Library of St. Mark's which Sansovino began and Scamozzi completed. To be properly appreciated they must be viewed from the natural element of Venice, the narrow lagoon waters. Then they become towering symbols of pomp and panoply. In Henry James's words, the Palazzo Rezzonico "reminds one from the low level of the gondola, of some broad-breasted mythological seahorse rearing up from the flood with

---

[1] Since this book was written R. Wittkower's long-awaited *Art and Architecture in Italy, 1600–1750* has been published. Like V. Golzio's *Seicento e Settecento*, it is an indispensable and exhaustive work of reference.

the toss of a sculptured crest and with emergent knees figured by the water steps".

Of Neapolitan Baroque architects the most compelling by far was the eighteenth-century Vanvitelli. To his major achievement, the Palace of Caserta with its tremendous staircase, I have devoted some space. But there were of course many others—Fanzago, Grimaldi, Picchiatti, Donzelli, Vaccaro, Sanfelice and Guglielmelli. Of these the best known, the most prolific and about the earliest in date is Cosimo Fanzago (1591–1678). He was the dominant architect in Naples for three-quarters of a century. He had a decided taste for perspective effects and his arcades and vaults are remarkable for their vertical impetus. He contributed more than anyone else to the colour that makes Neopolitan architecture so distinctive. His intro-duction of marble intarsia inlay—known as *pietre dure*—is nowhere more lavish than in the Church of the Convent of San Martino where it becomes almost oppressive. The senses are overwhelmed by the minute incrustations of marble upon pavement, walls and even roof. No-where can the eye find relief from the dizzy kaleidoscope of varie-gated colours; and, where there is no further room for marble, other precious materials, jasper, porphyry, mosaic and silver are used upon altars and the sacred furniture of sanctuaries.

When this polychrome decoration assumes the medium of maiolica in the next century the effect is more sympathetic. Every eye must rejoice in Giuseppe Donato's cloisters in the Convent of Santa Chiara. Here the garden is intersected with walks of which the vine draped pergolas and benches are lined with Capodimonte tiles. The octagonal columns are patterned with fruits and cornucopias in yellow and blue; the panels of the benches with coastal scenes, here a shipwreck, there classical ruins, and views of the Bay of Naples, Vesuvius, Etna, Scylla and Charybdis. A more delightful form of decoration cannot possibly be conceived. It found its way to cupolas and bell towers. No city of Italy was more redolent of colour than Naples. Even the plain walls of nondescript houses were washed with shades of mottled orange and apricot. As Harold Acton has written, the Baroque was the style that suited Naples; "it expressed itself like a swarm of nightingales released from a golden cage".[1]

Yet, when all is said and done, is Neapolitan architecture before the eighteenth century and the advent of Vanvitelli so very original? I am inclined to doubt it. The seventeenth-century Picchiatti's two churches of S. Agostino della Zecca and Monte della Misericordia alone depart from the old Counter-reformation, basilican type which had been discarded in Rome in the 1620s, but was still being copied in Naples by the dominant Fanzago school. The first of these churches on its terraced substructure of jewelled pilaster strips is singularly striking : the second, fashioned out of the towering palace of which its façade forms a part, is no less impressive. The fronts of both are imaginative. The interiors are unusual. That of the first has a wide nave connected to each aisle by three arches between architraved openings; that of the second is an early adaptation of Bernini's S. Andrea al Quirinale. Unless deliberately imitative, church plans in Naples generally were conventional. It is in decorative adjuncts that the magical beauties of Neapolitan churches reside— in the glowing ceiling panels of Corenzio and Solimena, the metal balustrades of choirs, the silver altars and silver reliquaries, the moulded stucco swags over side chapels, the intarsia ambries of "palissandro" wood in sacristies and of course in the lavish inlay of marble and other rare stones.

These decorative adjuncts do not, however, constitute Baroque architecture. Indeed the fantastic and the bizarre are not its proper constituents. For this reason the notorious Villa Palagonìa at Bagherìa in Sicily, though a creation of the eighteenth century, is no more Baroque than Wollaton Hall which was built by an Elizabethan tycoon in Nottinghamshire. It is eccentric surely; it is amusing; it may even be pretty. The huge saloon, with looking-glass ceiling of painted clouds and flights of birds over a golden balustrade adorned with urns, with walls of Coltonello marble from which polychrome busts of members of the Palagonìa family in periwigs lean and gesticulate like prisoners struggling to free themselves from bondage, is

[1] Harold Acton, *The Bourbons of Naples*, 1956.

grotesque. "All the chimneypieces, windows and sideboards", wrote an Irish contemporary[1] "are crowded with pyramids and pillars of teapots, candlecups, bowls, cups, saucers, etc., strongly cemented together; some of these columns are not without their beauty; one of them has a large china chamber-pot for its base, and a circle of pretty little flower-pots for its capital; the shaft of the column . . . is composed entirely of teapots". Apartments such as this are a separate, specialized study in the history of architectural decoration. They and the alarming array of statuary—buffoons, dwarfs and freaks—which Prince Palagonìa assembled in his garden have some accountable derivation which is not necessarily allied to art. No wonder that, as the same eyewitness wryly observed, "several living monsters have been brought forth in the neighbourhood".

Similarly the seventeenth- and eighteenth-century architecture of Apulia hardly subscribes to Baroque terms. The beautiful, soft honey stone of Lecce lent itself to the most facile carving. Francesco Zimbalo and Giuseppe Cino fairly encased surfaces with a welter of extravagant motifs, decorative but not functional. The structure beneath remained unaffected by Baroque figuration.

So I return to the vexed question: where and when does the Baroque begin and end? It was preceded by Mannerism which coincided roughly with the decline and painful revival of the Catholic Church after the shock of the Reformation, that is to say between the years 1520 and 1600. The Baroque, whose cradle was Ancient Rome and whose inspiration was the revived Faith, endured so long as artists were mindful of these two guiding factors. The moment they disregarded them the style ceased to satisfy the historic and religious needs of the people, and floundered. In Rome and the Papal States the reign of the Baroque fell more or less within the seventeenth century. It was superseded by the Rococo, a secular style which satisfied men's sensuous appetites only. For the Rococo is aesthetic, but not spiritual. It acknowledges no discipline and flaunts the canons of the Antique which shaped the physical structure of the Baroque style. The fully fledged Rococo made a first appear-

1 Pat Brydone, *Tour through Sicily and Malta in 1770*, published 1790.

ance in France about the year 1700 and reached Italy in modified form some twenty-five years later. It lingered in Europe until the finish of the third quarter of the eighteenth century.

Dates are, however, of small importance and merely act as useful punctuations to our memories. They are often misleading. So that when we speak of the Baroque flourishing in the Papal States between 1600 and 1700 we run the grave risk of being dogmatic. Besides we are not being strictly accurate. The Palazzo Madama[1], for instance, was built in 1642 and is still Mannerist, and not Baroque, in style. The west frontispiece of S. Maria Maggiore was built in 1750 and is Baroque, not Rococo. Certainly the end of the seventeenth century saw the Holy City's loss of leadership in architectural style. The Baroque scene was shifting to other Italian regions, notably Piedmont and to a lesser extent, Naples. At the same time the Baroque was coming into evidence in lands still more distant from Rome. It was expressing itself in strange foreign accents in Spain and Portugal, in Bavaria, Austria, the countries of Eastern Europe, and even in Latin America.

[1] The Palazzo Madama in Rome.

204

Bibliography

ARTICLES, CATALOGUES, LECTURES AND THESES, ETC.

Abercrombie, Patrick. "Maltese Baroque", *Architect and Building News*, 13 August 1943.

Accascina, Maria. "La Formazione artistica di Filippo Juvara", *Bolletino D'Arte*, 1, 11, 111, 1951–57.

Anonymous. "Arte Barocca", Article in *Enciclopedia Italiana*, 1930.

Anonymous. "Baroque", Article in *Chambers's Encyclopaedia*.

Ayscough, A. "Some Notes on Baroque Origins in Southern Italy", *Architectural Rev.*, August 1937.

Blunt, Anthony. "Mannerism in Architecture", *R.I.B.A. Journal*, March 1949.

Briggs, M. S. "Baroque Architecture", *R.I.B.A. Journal*, July 1913.

Calvesi, Maurizio. "La Chiesa e il Convento dei Celestini, Lecce", *Commentari*, 1954–55.

Connolly, Cyril. "Discovery and Praise of Rococo", *L'Œil*, 1955.

Coolidge, John. "Villa Giulia", *Art Bulletin*, 1943.

Coolidge, John. "Vignola and the Little Domes of St. Peter's", *Marsyas*, 11, 1942.

Fleming, John. "Malta, Naval Base of the Baroque", *Architectural Review*, June 1946.

Granger, Frank. "The Parthenon and the Baroque", *R.I.B.A. Journal*, October 1931.

Granger, Frank. "A Letter on Baroque", *Times Literary Supplement*, 15 March 1928.

Giavonnani, G. "Chiese della Seconda Metà del Cinquecento", *L'Arte*, XVI, 1913.

Guazzaroni, T. "Giovanni Milton in Italia", *Giornale Arcadico*, 1902.

Haskell, F. Thesis, *The Jesuits and the Fine Arts in Rome 1550–1700*, 1953.

Holford, W. G. "The Great Baroque Masquerade", *R.I.B.A. Journal*, January 1933.

Kimball, Fiske. "Creation of the Style of Louis XV", *Art Bulletin*, 1941.

Mahon, Denis, and Sutton, Denys. *Catalogue of Exhibition of Artists in 17th Century Rome*, 1955.

Martienssen, Heather. "The Nature of Baroque", I and II, *South African Architectural Record*, August 1950 and August 1952.

Martin, J. "Milton en Italie", *Bullet. Ital.*, X, 4, 1910.

Mauceri, E. "Facciata della Cattedrale di Siracusa", *L'Arte*, X (corr.), 1907.

Mauceri, E. "G. Serpotta", *L'Arte*, IV, 1901.

Mortimer, Raymond. "The Baroque", *London Mercury*, III, January 1921.

Moschini, V. "Le Architetture di Pietro da Cortona", *L'Arte*, XXIV, 1921.

Munoz, A. "La Scultura Barocca e l'Antico", *L'Arte*, XIX, 1916.

Nava, Antonia. "Antonio Raggi", *L'Arte*, XL, 1937.

Needham, John. "The Siting of Greek Buildings", *R.I.B.A. Journal*, March 1953.

Pevsner, N. "The Architecture of Mannerism", *The Mint*, 1946.

Pijoan, José. "Romanesque Baroque", *Art Bulletin*, 1926.

Pollak, O. "Borromini", biographical article in *Thieme-Becker*, 1910.

Sencourt, R. "Influence of Bernini on Wren", *Quarterly Review*, July 1942.

Sitwell, Osbert. "Noto a Baroque City", *Architectural Review*, October 1934.

Stockmeyer, E. "Art and Theory of Baroque", *Werk*, 1947.

Stone, Nicholas. "Diary of, in 1638", *Walpole Society*, vol. VII, 1917–18.

Swan, Michael. "Lecce the Florence of Baroque", *Geographical Magazine*, June 1952.

Toesca, Ilaria. "Alessandro Galilei in Inghilterra", *English Miscellany*, 1952.

Watkin, E. I. "Ecclesiastical Rococo", *Dublin Review*, 229, No. 467, 1955.

Watkin, E. I. "British Baroque", *Church Quarterly Review*, April 1946.

Webb, Geoffrey. "Baroque Art", lecture in *Proceedings of British Academy*, vol. XXXIII, 1947.

Wilkinson, L. P. "The Baroque Spirit in Ancient Art and Literature", *Trans. Roy. Soc. Lit.*, vol. XXV, 1950.

Wittkower, R. "Michelangelo's Biblioteca Laurenziana", *Art Bulletin*, 1934.

Wittkower, R. "Carlo Rainaldi and Roman Architecture of the Full Baroque", *Art Bulletin*, 1937.

Zeri, F. "The Pallavicini Palace in Rome", *Connoisseur*, November 1955.

BOOKS

Anonymous. *Horae Subsecivae: A Discourse of Rome*, 1620.

Argan, G. C. *Borromini*, 1952.

Baglione, G. *Vite de' pittore, scultori et architetti*, 1642.

Baldinucci, F. *Vita del Cavaliere G. L. Bernini*, 1682.

BIBLIOGRAPHY

Berkeley, Bishop G. *Journal of a Tour in Italy 1717, 1718.*

Blunt, Anthony. *Artistic Theory in Italy 1450–1600*, 1940.

Briganti, G. *Il Manierismo*, 1945.

Briggs, M. S. *Baroque Architecture*, 1913.

Brinckmann, A. E. *Theatrum Novum Pedemontii*, 1931.

Brion, Marcel. *Michel Ange*, 1939.

Brydone, P. *Tour through Sicily and Malta in 1770.*

Bryce, James. *Holy Roman Empire*, 1919.

Burnet, Bishop G. *Some Letters . . . from Italy*, etc., 1686.

Carden, R. W. *A Record of Michelangelo's Life as told in his Letters and Papers*, 1913.

Castyne, O. van de. *Question Rubens dans l'Histoire de l'Architecture.*

Chantelou, P. Fréart de. *Journal de Voyage en France du Cavalier Bernini*, 1930.

Clough, Arthur Hugh. *Letters from Rome: Amours de Voyage*, 1858.

Cismon, C. M. de V di Val, Rovere, L., Viale, V., and Brinckmann, A. E. *Filippo Juvara*, 2 vols., 1937.

Craven, Hon. Richard Keppel. *Tour through Southern Provinces of Naples*, 1821.

Croce, B. *Storia dell'età barocca in Italia* (Introduction), 1925.

D'Ors, Eugenio. *Du Baroque*, 1935.

Evelyn, John. *Diary* (in Italy), 1643–45.

Fischera, Francesco. *Giambattista Vaccarini*, 1935.

Fokker, T. H. *Roman Baroque Art*, 2 vols., 1938.

Fraschetti, S. *Bernini*, 1900.

Friedlaender, Walter. *Caravaggio Studies*, 1955.

Friedlaender, Walter, *Mannerism and Anti-Mannerism in Italian Painting*, 1958.

Giedion, S. *Space, Time and Architecture*, 1954.

Gothein, M. L. *A History of Garden Art*, 1928.

Goldscheider, L. *Michelangelo—Paintings, Sculptures, Architecture*, 1953.

Golzio, V. *Seicento e Settecento*, 1950.

Guarini, G. *Architettura Civile, 1668–1737.*

Hempel, E. *Borromini*, 1924.

Highet, Gilbert. *The Classical Tradition* (chs. 15 and 16), 1949.

Hübner, A von. *Life and Times of Sixtus V*, 1872.

Kaufmann, E. *Architecture in the Age of Reason*, 1955.

Kimball, Fiske. *Creation of the Rococo*, 1949.

Lang, P. H. *Music in Western Civilization*, 1942.

Lawrence, A. W. *Later Greek Sculpture*, 1927.

Magni, Giulio. *Il Barocca a Roma*, 1911.

Mahon, Denis. *Studies in Seicento Art and Theory*, 1947.

Mâle, Emile. *L'Art Religieux du Dix-Septième Siècle*, 1932.

Matthiae, G. *Ferdinando Fuga*, 1955.

Maugham, W. Somerset. *Don Fernando*, 1935.

Mayor, A. Hyatt. *The Bibiena Family*, 1945.

Molesworth, H. D. *Baroque Sculpture* (V. & A. Mus. publn.), 1954.

Montani, G. B. *I Cinque Libri*, etc., 1684.

Munoz, A. *Roma Barocca*, 1919.

Munoz, A. *Domenico Fontana*.

Munoz, A. *Francesco Borromini*, 1921.

Munoz, A. *Pietro da Cortona*, 1921.

Munoz, A. *Carlo Maderna*.

Oliveri, I. E. *Le Opere di B. A. Vittone*, 1920.

Pane, Roberto. *Bernini Architetto*, 1953.

Passeri, G. B. *Vite de' Pittori, scultori ed architetti . . . in Roma dal 1641–1673*, publ. 1772.

Pastor, Ludwig F. von. *History of the Popes*, vols. 25–31, 1939.

Perotti, M. V. *Borromini*, 1951.

Pevsner, N. *An Outline of European Architecture*, 1954.

Plutarch. "Pericles and 5th Century Art" (from *The Lives*).

Portoghesi, P. *Guarino Guarini*, 1956.

Pounelle and Bourdet. *St. Philip Neri and The Roman Society of His Times* (trs.), 1932.

Pozzo, Andrea. *Perspective* (trs. John James 1707), 1693.

Reymond, Marcel. *Le Bernin*, 1911.

Reymond, Marcel. *De Michel Ange à Tiepolo*, 1912.

Reynolds, Sir Joshua. *Thirteenth Discourse*, 1786.

Ricci, C. *Architettura Barocca in Italia*, 1911.

Rodocanachi, C. P. *Athens and the Greek Miracle*, 1948.

Rotili, Mario, *Filippo Raguzzini e il Rococo Romano*, 1955.

Rousset, Jean. *La Literature de l'Age Baroque en France*, 1954.

Saint-Non, Abbé de. *Voyage Pittoresque au Royaume des Deux Siciles*, 1786–87.

Scott, Geoffrey. *The Architecture of Humanism*, 1914.

Sedlmayr, H. *Die Architectur Borrominis*, 1924.

Shaftesbury, 3rd Earl of. *A Letter concerning the Art or Science of Design, written from Italy, 1712*.

Stokes, Adrian. *Michelangelo*, 1955.

Strzygowski, J. *The Origin of Christian Church Art*, 1923.

Swinburne, Henry. *Travel in the Two Sicilies*, 4 vols., 1785.

Symonds, J. A. *The Catholic Reaction*, 2 vols., 1886.

Tapié, Victor. *Baroque et Classicisme*, 1957.

Vasari, G. *Lives of the Painters*, etc.

Waterhouse, E. K. *Baroque Painting in Rome*, 1937.

Watkin, E. I. *Catholic Art and Culture* (chapter on "The Age of Baroque"), 1942.

Winckelmann, J. *History of Ancient Art*, vol. I (trs.), 1881.

Wittkower, R. *Bernini's Bust of Louis XIV*, 1951.

Wittkower, R. *Bernini, Sculptor of Roman Baroque*, 1955.

Wittkower, R. *Art and Architecture in Italy, 1600–1750*, 1958 (published since going to press).

Wölfflin, H. *Classical Art* (trs.), 1942.

Wölfflin, H. *Principles of Art History* (trs.), 1932.

Wölfflin, H. *Renaissance et Baroque* (trs. Marcel Reymond), 1908.

Index

The numerals in **bold type** refer to the figure numbers of illustrations.

216